Please remember that this is a library book,
and that it belongs only temporarily to each
person who uses it. Be considerate. Do
not write in this, or any, library book.

AFTER THE CIVIL WAR

By the author:
THE CIVIL WAR
AFTER THE CIVIL WAR

AFTER THE CIVIL WAR

A PICTORIAL PROFILE OF AMERICA FROM 1865 TO 1900

John S. Blay

BONANZA BOOKS • NEW YORK

*This book is dedicated to
the memory of my mother and father*

*This edition is published by Bonanza Books,
a division of Crown Publishers, Inc.
by arrangement with Thomas Y. Crowell Company*
b c d e f g h

Typography and layout by John S. Blay

Library of Congress Catalog Card No. 60-16582

Manufactured in the United States of America

FOREWORD

The Victorian period in American history was far from dull. The thirty-five years from the end of the Civil War to the turn of the century saw surge after surge of vigorous activity as the nation reached full manhood. Incoming immigrants enriched the collective blood stream of the country. Social habits were transformed because of inventions such as the incandescent electric light and the telephone. Under the capitalistic system, huge fortunes came into being. Labor organized rapidly to achieve a fair share of the high profits pouring into the nation's coffers. In the West, the frontier became a thing of the past as the Indians were tamed, the buffalo destroyed and the cattle drives checked. War with Spain made the United States a colonial power.

Contemporary Americans could follow their nation's progress through the copiously-illustrated periodicals of the day. *Harper's Weekly* produced full pictorial coverage of important events and personalities. *Scribner's Monthly, The Century Magazine* and *Frank Leslie's Illustrated Newspaper* contributed fine illustrations. Across the water, *The Illustrated London News* showed a lively interest in American events and kept staff artists busy recording them.

Pictures from the publications mentioned, especially those from *Harper's,* form the basis of this volume; they have been supplemented by illustrations from other periodicals and books of the period. My thanks are hereby expressed to the editors and picture editors of the Victorian newspapers and magazines. They left behind a rich storehouse of graphic information.

Henry Chafetz and S. B. Solomon were of immense help in finding pictures and research material for this book; their work was supplemented by contributions from Paul Porter and Vincent Mercaldo. Frederick Petzoldt lent his technical skill in helping process the pictures for reproduction. From the time the book was conceived until its completion, Joanne Palmer was a constant source of suggestion and encouragement.

August 5, 1960   J. S. B.

CONTENTS

Reconstruction

WAR'S AFTERMATH

2

3

The Year of Victory Saw a Severely Battered Nation
In the Process of Binding Up Its Painful Wounds

GAUNT chimneys, fire-blackened buildings, acres of rubble were everywhere. The cause was lost and the South crushed in 1865. Good and brave men who perished in hundreds of thousands for an idea were not yet history; they lay too newly dead.

Desolation and despair became the portion of Richmond, Atlanta, Columbia, Charleston, Vicksburg, and Mobile. Georgia and South Carolina bore Sherman's mark. Sheridan's trail of fire forced bitter penance on the Shenandoah Valley farmers whose teeming produce had fed the men of Longstreet and Lee. The silos were gone, and the corn rotted in the fields.

Southern veterans, in the months after Appomattox, wandered dusty country roads in search of wives and children who had fled the terrible Union forces. In the North, men maimed by battle wore their faded blues as they restlessly roamed from town to town hawking salve, soap, notions, and patent medicines (left).

The Civil War preserved the Union but in so doing, shook the nation to its roots. Nothing could ever be quite the same. In the wake of blood came bitterness, hatred, vindictiveness, and an ugly concept of race relations which has never disappeared.

Multiple troubles, both physical and spiritual, fell on the states which had defied Federal power. An entire class, and the aristocratic way of life it personified, was gone. Without the rulers, there was no rule and civil government all but vanished. Compounding the confusion was an enormous new social class: 3½ million newly freed and bewildered Negroes looking for direction and guidance.

Debt stalked the South, whose economy floated on a sea of worthless paper currency. Banks were closed, railroads ravaged, cotton presses burned. Barnacles flourished along the empty wharves of seaport cities. Union soldiers camped in the fields.

To the victorious North fell the formidable tasks of stitching the nation together again, integrating blacks and whites and preventing mistreatment of former slaves, re-establishing the southern economy and providing for restoration of local governments. Despite high taxes, debt and inflation, the North was rich in material things. Contractors had made a good thing out of the war and a newly rich middle class was emerging. But portions of the North were spiritually sick. Northern fire-eaters called for lasting vengeance against the treasonable states. Manufacturers, looking at the peace in a colder light, were determined to eliminate the planter class which had espoused low tariffs. Politicians, to maintain themselves in office, nursed and kept alive prejudice.

The ultimate tragedy of Reconstruction was lack of leadership. In a time that cried out for greatness, only mediocrity appeared. The tall man lay in his tomb and his successor could not match his shadow.

President Andrew Johnson sat in an uneasy chair. Honest, pugnacious, willing, he was, after a brief false start, sincerely devoted to Lincoln's dream of a soft peace as the only logical road to reunion and understanding. Johnson toiled valiantly for his cause but was no match for the "hard war" men who dominated Congress. At their door lay the blame for the dismal period known as the Reconstruction Era.

5

As a Vengeful Congress Killed the Dream of a Soft Peace,

Sumner (*left*) was brilliant, Stevens (*right*) dogged and ambitious. Together they made a team which ground down Johnson's power and set a group of campaign-hardened Union generals (*below*) to rule the South. Among the occupying troops were many Negroes.

The Conquered South Settled Down to Military Occupation

PRESIDENT Andrew Johnson (*above*) was a tough, self-taught man who reached the highest office in the land after serving in state and Federal governments and functioning as military governor of Tennessee. It was his intention to maintain the power Lincoln had given the executive branch. But Congress had its fill of executive strength. Radical Republicans, calling for a tough peace and immediate Negro suffrage, rallied their forces and went for Johnson's throat. Their leaders were Senator Charles Sumner of Massachusetts and Representative Thaddeus Stevens of Pennsylvania.

Lincoln had vetoed the Wade-Davis bill, a "hard peace" measure, set up qualifications under which former Confederate states could enter the Union again, and established provisional governments in Virginia, Tennessee, Arkansas, and Louisiana. Johnson followed suit, creating provisional governments in the remaining states: North Carolina, South Carolina, Mississippi, Georgia, Texas, Alabama, and Florida. In December 1865, Congress refused to seat the representatives of the "Johnson governments."

This was a bid to trim executive power, prevent immediate southern anti-Negro legislation, and make the House and Senate Republican bastions secure against encroaching southern Democrats. Congress then established a Joint Committee on Reconstruction, heavily loaded with Radicals, which proposed a new amendment to the Constitution.

The Fourteenth Amendment guaranteed citizenship rights to every person born or naturalized in the U.S.A., reduced representation in Congress of any state that refused the vote to Negroes, disqualified Confederate leaders from holding state or Federal office, and affirmed the U.S. war debt while repudiating that of the Confederacy. Tennessee speedily ratified and was brought back into the Union; the other ten southern states rejected the measure because of the disqualifying clause.

In retaliation, the Radicals pushed through the Reconstruction Act of March 2, 1867 (later supplemented), dividing the ten guilty states into five military districts, under Union generals. Occupying forces set up constitutional conventions.

The constitutions so created, which provided for Negro suffrage, were to be submitted to Congress. Voters were to elect state legislatures pledged to ratify the Fourteenth Amendment. In due time and after much trouble, the amendment was ratified.

The Fifteenth Amendment was ratified as well. It forbade any state to deny the vote because of "race, color, or previous condition of servitude."

7

On February 25, 1868, Thaddeus Stevens, ill and nearly dead, gave formal notice of the impeachment of Andrew Johnson at the bar of the Senate. The shabby and vindictive incident, first of its kind in United States history, marked a low point in Reconstruction.

A Bitter Roman Holiday at Andrew Johnson's Expense

JOHNSON'S belligerence, integrity, and forthright use of the veto so antagonized his opponents that they set a trap for his downfall with the Tenure of Office Act in March 1867, which forbade the President to remove any officeholder without Senate consent. Johnson, fully aware of the consequences, obliged by suspending Secretary of War Edwin M. Stanton, a Radical.

Three days later, the House voted to impeach Johnson for "high crimes and misdemeanor." Trial was set before the Senate, and it lasted two months. When the prosecution's main point failed to hold water legally, it became evident the entire affair was a trumped-up scandal.

Nevertheless, only one vote saved the victim, who was acquitted after seven Republicans joined the Democratic minority.

Hysterical crowds watched impeachment proceedings from Senate galleries (*top*) as newspapermen raced to file their hot copy.

10

Northern Humanitarians, Sorely Touched by the Plight of Former Slaves, Moved to Bring Them Aid

THE NEWLY freed slave was a pathetic figure. Uneducated, conditioned to the plantation system, he confused his precious new freedom with the right to unlimited idleness. The phantom promise of "forty acres and a mule" to each man led to a kind of shaky optimism.

To lend a hand in this situation, many private charities and organizations from the North moved in. Officially, the Negro was to be protected by the Freedmen's Bureau, which had been set up during Lincoln's lifetime. Under Major General Oliver O. Howard, the Freedmen's Bu-

reau was established to last one year after the end of the war; eventually, it operated for more than four years.

Branch offices were established in Memphis (*upper left*) and other southern cities. Former slaves brought their problems to the Bureau. Its major tasks were coordinating the work of private organizations and making sure Negroes were not exploited. The Bureau also had a hand in land distribution. Allotment of food and medicines was a Bureau function, as was the establishment of schools such as the one shown (*lower left*) at Vicksburg.

Freedmen's Bureau schools were often burned in the course of ugly race riots which swept Memphis, New Orleans, and other cities throughout 1866. When colored troops began drinking heavily and accosting the sensitive southern whites, the tinder was laid for firing.

"The First Vote" was a famed sentimental picture of 1867, popular in the North, although there existed many ardent abolitionists who felt the Negro was not yet ready for the franchise. In 1870 and 1871, Negro rights were further protected by the Enforcement Acts.

Political, Not Humanitarian, Reasons Made It That Way

WITH the vote, the Negro became a political force, to be manipulated by carpetbaggers (northern opportunists seeking their fortunes in the South) and scalawags (white southerners who favored the Radicals). At the constitutional conventions set up under military rule in southern states, Negroes played an important part and were often in the majority.

Untrained, at sea when confronted by sharp-talking politicians, the Negroes used their votes as directed and in many cases precipitated a sea of pork barrel legislation in the new state governments. The constitutions themselves, many modeled on those of northern states, were surprisingly good in their planks on universal suffrage, education, and taxation. It was in the state governments as they operated from day to day that the evils emerged.

Led by the opportunistic carpetbaggers, legislatures voted huge sums for public works projects which feathered everyone's nest, set up bars and restaurants for their own comfort, floated enormous loans, and otherwise saddled the taxpayers with debt.

Stung into action, southerners retaliated with night-riding societies like the Ku Klux Klan (page 1), dedicated to frightening the Negroes and driving out the alien northerners. By 1877, southern whites once again controlled their local governments.

Legislation in South Carolina's House of Representatives was often an erratic affair because, the southerners said, Negroes were in the majority at the capital. This situation declined after 1872 when the Amnesty Act restored some privileges to former Confederates.

13

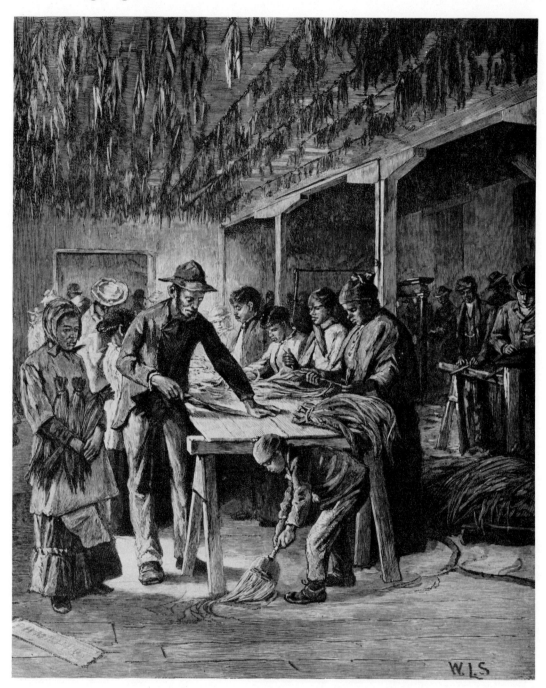

Tobacco stripping, pictured above at Danville, Virginia, began again as soon as the postwar crops were harvested. During the Civil War, Union soldiers had swapped coffee for southern tobacco and acquired a taste for the leaf; their demand provided a market for crops.

14

THE END of the planter class brought death to the great plantations of the South, but the society remained agrarian in the decade following the war. Cash was scarce. In an effort to plant and harvest cotton and other crops as best they could, the landowners evolved the share-crop system. Under this, the former slaves and poor whites traded their labor for a share of the crops they grew. The planter supplied seed, fertilizer, draft animals, and often food and housing; the laborer gave his toil. When the crop was in, the worker turned over half or one-third of it to the planter and kept the rest for himself.

The system was far from ideal but it worked in a time of crisis. Money-lenders who helped finance the arrangements usually insisted on cotton or tobacco (for they were easy to sell) in the fields, and so limited the South to a narrow economy.

Over the years, the great reaches of land were broken up. Middle class farmers saw a chance to get land at bargain prices. Big estates went by the boards, and in twenty years, the number of farms in the former Confederacy had more than doubled.

Cotton (*above*) remained king but it was more than a decade before the fields reached their prewar production. In the meantime, processing of cotton became a leading Dixie industry. Cheap water power, an abundance of low-priced labor, and proximity to the raw material brought textile mills down from their traditional locations in New England. So began the mill villages.

From 1880 on, the "New South" emerged, based not only on cotton and tobacco, but also on furniture built from southern pine, increased cultivation of rice and sugar cane, and a burgeoning industry in citrus fruits.

15

Rich Natural Resources, Inexpensive Power, and Lack
Of Labor Unions Brought Industry to the New South

Richmond's Tredegar Iron Works, which had labored on munitions throughout the war, became a part of the new industrial South. Discoveries of coal and iron deposits and restoration of rail lines created the big iron and steel plants in Alabama and Tennessee.

Everyday Life

HOME AND FAMILY

THE YEARS following the Civil War were rich ones in the North and showed abundant evidence of material prosperity. There was a fresh crop of millionaires; there was, as always, a depressed group. But the upper middle class was in the ascendancy, helping the nation burst its seams.

The prosperous family (*left*) seemed the epitome of American culture and achievement. America was still a patriarchy. Father was supreme. His arrival at home from counting house or shop signaled a minor celebration each day. Children appeared from their upstairs playroom, the doting wife was in attendance, and servants offered refreshment to take the edges off the ten-hour day he had worked.

In the big cities, well-to-do families lived in tall, narrow homes such as the Boston edifice shown at right. The first, or semibasement floor, "below stairs," held the kitchen and workrooms. The front door usually led into a hall, embellished with umbrella stands, coat trees and a mirror framed in golden oak. Off the hall were the parlor, sitting room, and sometimes the dining room. The upper floors held bedrooms, sewing rooms, and the nursery, and servants lived on the floor just under the eaves. Many builders faced these dwellings with a rough brown sandstone and the name "brownstone" became generic to all houses of this type.

Hot air or steam heated the city domiciles and they were lit by kerosene lamps or gas fixtures. Daily deliveries of ice, wood, and coal supplied refrigerators and kitchen stoves.

Interiors were heavily carpeted and curtained, overdecorated, and presumably stuffy and depressing to modern tastes. But servants were cheap, food was plentiful, and the material evidences of prosperity existed everywhere.

Life in these formidable dwellings reportedly ran on a strict schedule, based on the habits and needs of the head of the house. The colonial maxim of "early to bed and early to rise" still held sway for a good reason: the working day was a long one for both man and wife. The latter, despite her servants, ran her home as a captain runs a ship.

PURSUIT of man by maid was a necessary preliminary to the establishment of a solid Victorian family. Victory in the chase called for a blissful honeymoon at such American resorts as White Sulphur Springs (*above*) or Niagara Falls (*right*). Confronted with a scene such as the one pictured on this page, caption writers of the 1880s went all to pieces:

"An idyl of complacency, of beatitude. Stress and storm there might have been, but now the calm haven of happiness has been reached. The perfect repose of the lady shows that, as does the man's assured look of possession. He might seem nonchalant, and yet the line of vision from his eyes is direct. Perhaps they had to wait so long—so long before they were man and wife. He takes to the mint julep as to the manner born. . . . He may then with his elbow give the hammock the slightest impulse,

so as not to endanger the fruit-laden table. . . . And it had all come to pass; and now she wonders how it all did happen. Oh! the joy of it, and as she swings and swings, those loving eyes of hers, beneath their fringe of lashes, may seem half drowsy, yet there is a brown flash in them as they seek her husband's glance. Even were her eyes dormant, the smile on her lips tells her heart's story."

To achieve a reverie such as the above, some brisk wooing was called for. It was a sentimental era, one which made famous the lace-paper valentine. The Victorian belle exploited sentiment to the full. In her arsenal were ribbons and ruffles, the ability to blush, and a thorough knowledge of fudge making.

Sentiment persisted but the Civil War stereotype of a lawn-clad maiden who fainted dead away at the first sign of emotion disappeared. In her place was the comradely girl.

20

Before Settling Down to Create Personal Dynasties, Victorian Couples Enjoyed Carefree Honeymoons

Her opportunities for romance depended on where she lived. City girls, considered "fast" by their country cousins, were taken to concerts, opera, and the theater, and the evening occasionally worked up to a grand climax with a champagne and oyster supper after the entertainment, or a chafing-dish feast at the lady's residence.

Carriage rides, skating parties, bicycle trips, or excursions by trolley or steamboat gave young lovers their chances for limited intimacy if they could evade their omnipresent chaperons. The epitome of refined love-making was reached when a young man, overcome by moonlight on the water, murmured a few tasteful lines from *Thanatopsis* to his beloved.

Dancing flourished. The polka, galop, and waltz were most intimate; the German, the quadrille, and the Virginia reel brought groups together. Country dances, following corn shucking or apple picking, proved to be zesty affairs, shaking wooden floors and bringing down dust from the farmhouse ceilings.

Rural courting took advantage of snow-covered roads for group sleigh rides; in summer, the hay ride was a welcome substitute. Canoeing on river or lake was a favorite pastime of bucolic swains. In both city and country, indoor games ranked high as a pastime for mixed groups. Blindman's buff, proverbs, cat and mouse, hunt the slipper, and wiggles titillated the company. And there was always the candy pull. The means were simple but effective, and the determined girl got her man.

The Newly Married Couple Often Began in a Cottage
But Soon Developed a Taste for Grander Architecture

· Plan · of · First · Floor ·

RESIDENCE OF ~
C:T:YERKS:ESQ
MICHIGAN:AVE:
CHICAGO:

BVRLING & WHITEHOVSE
ARCHITECTS:

In an effort to create sumptuous effects, designers of Victorian homes embellished flat surfaces with a multiplicity of useless ornaments. Stained-glass windows, iron grillwork, crenelated walls, balustrades, and miniature porches clamored and fought for attention.

22

OUPLES starting life together in big cities often had to depend on boardinghouses, although apartments appeared in increasing numbers during the 1880s and 1890s. In the suburbs, and in smaller towns, houses were available in every price bracket.

The home shown below, known as a "cottage" in Victorian parlance, could be built for $2,500. Made of pine, it had three bedrooms and a bath and provided a suitable nest for a fledgling family. The home shown has the virtue of simplicity but this was not universal, even in low-priced homes. The jigsaw killed the clean lines of these modest cottages. Fretwork and assorted gingerbread, pasted on with no rhyme or reason, cre-

ated a Hansel-and-Gretel appearance.

As the family grew, and its income increased, a substantial home in brick or stone became the goal. Solidly built, a lasting investment, such a pseudo-palace as the one shown at left became a status symbol. In structures such as these, costing $15,000 and more, architects ran riot.

There was little or no native architecture. Instead, a crop of Gothic chateaus, Italian villas and Moorish temples appeared. Exaggerated roofs, useless cupolas, turrets, columns, buttresses and chimneys encrusted the frames of these expensive dwellings. The Victorian period marked the nadir of domestic building in the United States.

The saving grace of late nineteenth-century architecture often lay in the ground on which it was built. Even the plots occupied by small cottages were sufficiently large to admit shade trees, lawns, and flowering bushes to soften the lines of buildings and rest the eye.

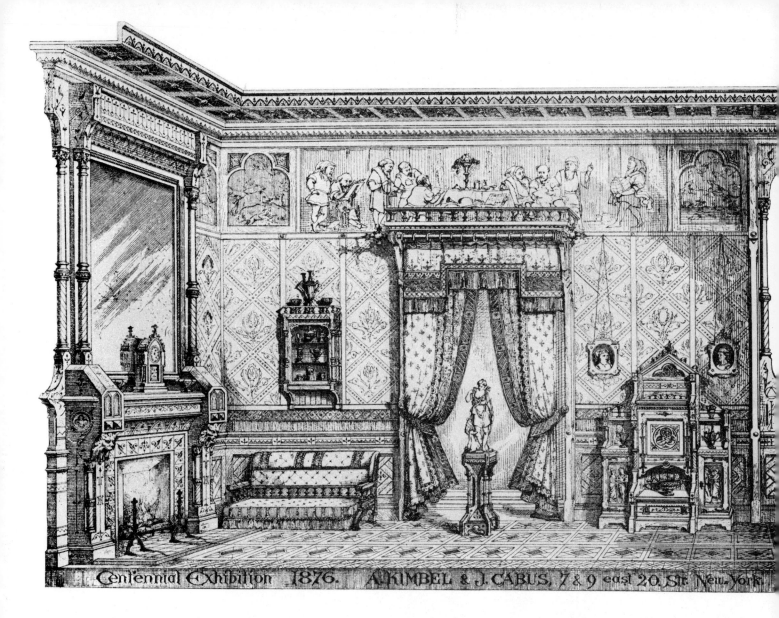

Centennial Exhibition 1876. A. KIMBEL & J. CABUS, 7 & 9 east 20. St. New York.

THE EXTERIORS of Victorian homes were bad; the interiors worse. There was one basic rule: leave no surface uncluttered. Heavily figured papers covered walls which were rich with mirrors, bookcases, and steel engravings in oversize frames. Cornices and ceilings carried intricate patterns. Thick portieres marked doorways and bulky draperies half covered windows, effectively keeping out daylight.

The gloomy rooms held furniture which was heavy and ponderous, giddily carved with superfluous ornament. Mahogany, oak, and walnut were favored. Shiny black horsehair covered couches and chair seats. Upholstery was plush or velvet in turkey red, saffron yellow, or poison green.

Picture albums, china dogs, painted pillows, mandolins, porcelain figurines, and such confections as the bonbon dish shown at upper right, made of coral and sea shells, existed in profusion. Painted plates, fanciful Bavarian beer mugs, and brass candle holders added welcome notes of richness. The problem of dusting a Victorian living room staggers the imagination.

Almost every well-ordered home held a sentimental piece of sculpture called a Rogers group (*upper right*), and contained a study holding the family library (*right*).

24

THE CHARITY PATIENT

25

26

Men's Clothes Were Dull and Conservative from 1865 To 1900, but Paris and London Dictated Feminine Attire

FASHIONABLE ladies of the late nineteenth century looked across the sea for inspiration, to the house of Worth and other great designers. In the United States, *Godey's Lady's Book, Peterson's Magazine,* and *Harper's Bazar* reported the latest from Europe, illustrated with elaborate costume plates.

The biggest fashion news was the decline of the hoop skirt and the pyramidal figure it had created, after the Civil War, and the rise in popularity of the bustle and the flowing drapery it supported. Contrary to nature and an obvious distortion, the bustle waxed and waned in popularity. In some years it was an elaborate affair, in others a mere patch of padding, but it remained a part of fashionable costume. The vagaries of style may be traced roughly on the opposite page which shows (*left to right, top to bottom*) a pyramidal house dress of 1867, an evening dress of 1874, a summer afternoon dress of 1878, and walking costumes of 1881. The tall, slender beauty (*right*) of the 1890s was properly wasp-waisted and gently padded.

The vogue of the tiny waist meant torture in the form of heavy corsets which pushed up the bosom and narrowed the middle, then expanded to permit graceful curves over the hipline. Frequent fainting spells were caused by constriction of blood supply and pressure on the internal organs. Suffering as they did, and carrying a superfluity of cloth, American girls of the later Victorian decades still managed to be fresh and beautiful.

Piled-up elaborate coiffures of great weight somewhat balanced the bustles. Braids and chignons were gradually replaced by simple hair arrangements as the century ended.

27

RICH AND POOR

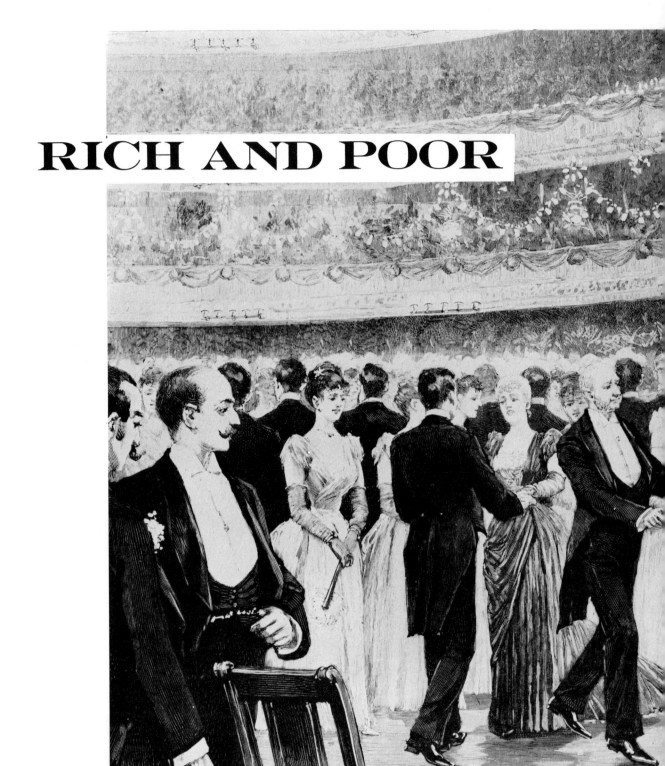

29

In Less Than 100 Years the United States Created a Wealthy Class Which Set Standards for the Nation

WHEN Ward McAllister, shown at right attired for a costume ball, told Mrs. William Astor there were only four hundred people worth knowing, he named the new American society. Journalists picked up "the four hundred" and used it frequently as they chronicled the daily revels of the exclusive few.

This was a parvenu society, based not on title or landed estates, but on the naked power of money. The new social arbiters were very rich and showed off their multimillion-dollar fortunes with ostentation. New York was the center of dazzle and glitter.

The young were taken in hand early (*left*) to make sure the social graces were properly infused. Their parents could be seen nightly at the prime showcase, the Metropolitan Opera House (*lower left*).

A welcome refuge from social rounds came with the introduction of exclusive men's clubs (*below*).

Elaborate Summer Playgrounds Along the Atlantic Coast

THE NEW YORK social season reached its peak in a series of climaxes such as the Metropolitan Opera Ball on New Year's Eve (pages 28-29). As the winter season ended, society's leading hostesses laid their summer plans.

The most famous resort was Newport, Rhode Island, a town dating from pre-Revolutionary days. A row of fancy mansions soon dominated the little town, and their inhabitants took the sun and air on the nearby beach (*right*).

Long Island was nearer home, and boasted a series of rich and exclusive summer colonies. Scions of the wealthy families could indulge their penchant for the expensive and exciting game of polo at such places as the Rockaway Hunting Club (*below*).

Perhaps the supreme summer sport was yachting (*left*). Steam and sail-powered vessels were abundant.

On the Other Side of the Social Coin Were the Poor Who Lived Out Their Lives in Misery and Despair

THE RICH were few and powerful, the poor many and helpless, in the generation which followed the Civil War. Gradual closing of the frontier and the Panic of 1873 tended to increase the number of the unfortunate.

Poverty-stricken families huddled in the tenements of New York, Boston, and other big cities. From 10 to 20 per cent of these cities' people dwelled in substandard houses lacking plumbing, running water, heat, light, and air. Stifling summer nights saw the masses gather on the docks seeking river breezes to ease their discomfort (*below*). In the winter, threats of eviction for nonpayment of rent (*right*) haunted the family wage earners.

The crowded slums were breeders of disease. Typhoid, scarlet fever, cholera, smallpox, and tuberculosis burst forth again and again in epidemic proportions in the cities.

Crusading journalists like Jacob Riis helped expose these evils toward the end of the century. Church groups, welfare agencies and political organizations moved in to help.

RETAIL TRADE

ONE OF the major business phenomena of the nineteenth century was emergence of the big-city department store, an institution which changed the shopping habits of millions. In the past, shops had carried a single line of goods, as exemplified in the Boston jewelry store shown below. This was the European custom.

About the time of the Civil War, far-seeing merchants began to create places of business offering a variety of goods and services. By the end of the century, a Victorian lady could spend her allowance on hosiery, notions, cutlery, children's clothes, and furniture—all under one roof (*opposite page*).

The spiritual father of the new system was Irish-born Alexander T. Stewart whose Tenth Street retail store in New York, built in 1862, was the biggest in the world, covering an area of two acres. It was later sold to John Wanamaker who, along with R. H. Macy, was in the forefront of the new line of merchant princes.

A. T. Stewart was a man of many virtues and boundless energy. Wholesaler, retailer, hotel man, city planner, he was one of the first of the big millionaires in the U.S.A.

Despite New Department Stores the Nineteenth-century
Housewife Still Went to Market for Many Purchases

HUGE open-air markets for food were a part of every metropolis (*left*). Copied after such European institutions as Les Halles in Paris, they offered tempting displays of fish, poultry, meat, game, and fruits and vegetables in season. Daily or semiweekly shopping was necessary because indifferent systems of home refrigeration left much to be desired.

Rural people raised much of their own food and depended on the general store for staples and the traveling peddler (*lower left*) for furbelows and gossip. These itinerant merchants roved from farm to farm with their stocks of city-made goods, bringing news of isolated areas.

The jam-packed carts were slowly displaced after 1870 with the advent of the big mail order houses geared to meet the farmer's needs. Montgomery Ward began in 1872; Sears, Roebuck and Company in 1886. Their enormous catalogues, packed with treasure, became prize possessions in every farmhouse.

Enterprising retailers made their wares known through a miniature art form known as the Victorian trade card (*right*). Adorned with mawkish children and sickly puns, chromolithographed in hideous colors, these were passed out in the street and dropped into mail slots.

Nineteenth-century Advertising in Newspapers and Magazines Had a Simple and Direct Charm All Its Own

A corset must

Fit to Wear

Dr. Warner's
Coraline Corsets
are fitted to
living models.

ADVERTISING was direct and hard-hitting. There was no such thing as the "soft sell." Men who bought space hawked their products in no uncertain terms.

Advertisers paid little attention to Victorian prudery. Sex was an enticement, as shown by the Pears' Soap lady above, bathing in sybaritic Roman splendor. Intimate garments were pictured shamelessly (*left*) and often carried endorsements from people prominent in public life. As always, the exotic had its own appeal (*right*).

Perhaps the biggest single trend in late nineteenth-century advertising was built around the wonders of electricity. Electric combs, hairbrushes, corsets, and garters were lavishly described.

Horrific children, horses wearing head warmers, and talking dogs were common, but such pleasant idiocies were balanced by simple local ads which were often tiny masterpieces of Victorian typography (*upper right*).

40

SPIRITUAL LIFE

The Legacy of Faith Left by the Founding Fathers Was

Symbolizing the growing strength of the Catholic Church in the U.S.A. during the late Victorian period was St. Patrick's Cathedral on New York's Fifth Avenue. Begun in 1858, the huge Gothic structure was completed twenty years later and dedicated in 1879.

Still a Strong Force in Late Nineteenth-century America

MID-VICTORIAN America was strongly religious and rigidly Protestant. The middle class of the large cities and the majority of rural dwellers embraced Methodism or worshiped as Baptists or Presbyterians. These three sects made up two-thirds of the 72,000 church congregations existing in 1870. There were splinter groups, broken off from these main sources, and a host of other faiths as well, in the Protestant camp.

Sunday was a solemn day over the reaches of the United States. Adults did only necessary chores, and kept the Sabbath sacred. Children, brushed and scrubbed, were pushed off to special services followed by Sunday School and evening devotions. But religion was not always cold and sober.

Beating the drum for their own personal evangelism, Dwight L. Moody and Ira D. Sankey barnstormed the U.S.A. and Europe as Protestantism's most colorful standard-bearers. Their huge revival meetings, held in halls and amphitheaters (pages 42-43) brought out audiences in thousands to hear the doctrines of conversion and redemption. Moody was a glowing speaker with a warm personal manner. Sankey played the organ and led choral groups. Although frowned upon by many, they left a colorful imprint on the religious scene.

With the flowing tides of immigration, practitioners of the older European faiths poured into the country. The largest of this group was the Catholic congregation. By 1900, there were 9 million Roman Catholics in the United States, most of them in the large cities. The majority came from Ireland, Italy, and Germany.

Jewish immigration also was strong and steady, from Russia, Austria, Ger-

many, and Poland. In the 1890s, some 25,000 Jews per year came through the port of New York, and their colorful ceremonies (*above*) soon became a part of the nation's religious life.

As the Century Drew to a Close There Was an
Impressive Outburst of Humanitarian Activity

The drive for woman suffrage succeeded, within limits, in many sections. These Boston ladies, voting at a municipal election, exemplified partial victory. In other cities, women voted on taxes, bond issues, growing school problems, and such matters of local interest.

Causes bloomed like spring flowers as a result of determined women, dedicated men, and dawning social conscience. Care of the indigent, the insane, and the young improved through the work of private agencies and religious groups.

Reform drives were spearheaded by such vigorous feminists as Carrie Chapman Catt, Elizabeth Cady Stanton and Susan B. Anthony. Especially vociferous in their demand for the vote, they were aided by such national figures as Henry Ward Beecher.

Professions such as nursing drew feminine recruits (*right*). Women lawyers were hanging out their shingles, as were doctors. Females invaded the ministry and social-work agencies.

The distaff side joined forces behind the courageous Henry Bergh, founder of the Society for the Prevention of Cruelty to Animals, which produced such innovations as the horse ambulance (*below*) for draft animals.

NEW YORK

National Temperance Society & Publication House,

No. 172 WILLIAM STREET.

DEMON rum was always under fire from ardent advocates of temperance who distributed tracts (*left*) by the million and introduced novelties such as the portable coffee stand (*below*), aimed at keeping the honest workman outside the swinging doors. Liquor was big business and produced sizable government income through the taxes it paid. Fighting the interests were the national Prohibition Party (1869), the Women's Christian Temperance Union (1874), and the Anti-Saloon League of America (1895).

The downfallen, brought to their state through liquor, poverty, or crime, sought help at missions which were springing up in big cities to offer food and shelter (*right*). Pioneering in this field was the American branch of the Salvation Army under Commander Ballington Booth and his wife (*lower right*).

EDUCATION

A BURGEONING population, increasing prosperity, and the growing respect for knowledge sent the number of students in the United States soaring after the Civil War. From the snug one-room schoolhouses of the prairies (*below*) to the august halls of Princeton (*left*), teachers were faced with larger student bodies.

Some 7 million attended elementary school in 1870. The number had risen to more than 16 million by the turn of the century. In that time high school enrollment rose from 161,000 to 700,000. Students in college reached 50,000 per year shortly after the war; by 1900 the number was 238,000.

This was a vigorous period in the field of American education. Most of the excitement was at the top, at the college and professional-school level. In the wide areas of the Midwest and Far West, elementary education remained a somewhat hit-or-miss affair. There were no grades in the old frame schoolhouses. Farm boys and girls stumbled through the simple fundamentals of the three R's until their parents put them to work on the land. Teachers averaged salaries of $300 to $400 per year. While the quantity of elementary schools increased, their quality remained mediocre.

Things were better in the field of high schools. Public funds, once used only for free elementary schools, were diverted for high school construction and staffing. By 1880, there were more than eight hundred such institutions in the land. They blossomed because western pioneers had fixed ideas about the need for free education on the secondary-school level for those who could not afford the expensive, private eastern academies. Under the aegis of state university training programs, the caliber of high school teachers improved.

52

A Series of Progressive Events Brought New Vitality to The American College Scene over the Course of 35 Years

FOR DECADES, the college system of the United States had stagnated. A new lease on life came after the Civil War with implementation of the Morrill Act of 1862, the founding of new colleges, increased attention to higher education for women and creation of Negro colleges.

The Morrill Act gave each state large tracts of land to endow a college for instruction in the agricultural and mechanical arts. Educators started from the ground up, often in the face of ridicule, to teach such subjects as agriculture, but succeeded in time. The "landgrant" colleges such as Pennsylvania State became a prominent part of the national scene.

Wealthy philanthropists kept the flame burning with donations such as that which began Johns Hopkins University at Baltimore in 1876, an outstanding institution for graduate study. Ezra Cornell gave half a million dollars which, combined with the land-grant endowment, created the famed university bearing his name (*left*) in 1868. In the Far West, railroad man Leland Stanford submitted plans for a college (*below*) at Palo Alto, California, in memory of his son. It was chartered in 1885 and opened in 1891.

Hard on the heels of the Civil War came Vassar Female College at Poughkeepsie, N.Y., to be followed in 1875 by establishment of Wellesley and Smith (*lower left*) for the elevation and edification of young ladies. In the Midwest, coeducation was accepted as normal and desirable.

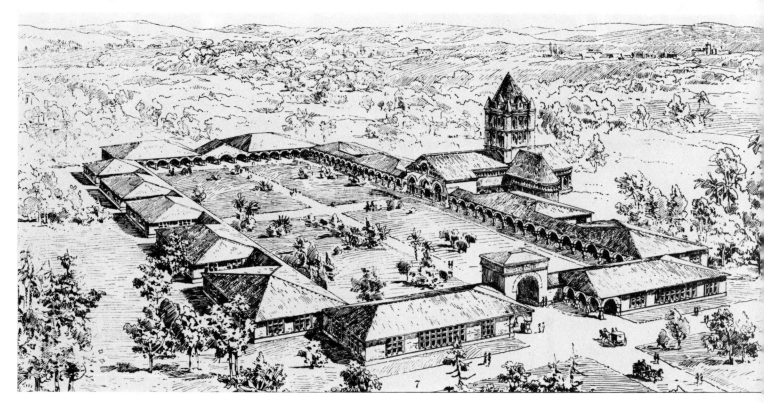

IT WAS the great good fortune of the United States to find a group of college presidents, in the late 1800s, who showed uncompromising standards of quality and immense breadth of vision and imagination. Because of their persistent efforts, stale and outmoded curricula were junked in favor of flexible study plans, and the quality of graduate schools was immeasurably improved.

A sound liberal education was hard to come by in 1865; there was nothing in the U.S.A. to compare with the careful and thorough scholastic systems of the Continent. American students had little choice in their courses. Ancient classics, classical languages, declamation, and a smattering of philosophy was the portion of the undergraduate. College rules held him to that sparse fare and even if his desire for more exotic knowledge was strong, little of it was offered.

The revolution began with the establishment of an elective system under which the student had a wide freedom of choice among courses, and the crea-

tion of new studies geared to the modern world. Among the pioneers in the battle for more liberal education were Charles W. Eliot, made president of Harvard in 1869, and Andrew D. White, who reached the same office at Cornell in 1867. James McCosh of Princeton contributed his salty Scotch views to the fight which was strongly championed in the Midwest by the University of Michigan's James B. Angell.

By 1876, Daniel C. Gilman became president of Johns Hopkins, imposing new and severe standards for those who sought graduate studies. Under Gilman, the university became famous as a training ground for teachers and medical students. The graduate schools at Harvard, Yale, and Columbia looked at their requirements for degrees with critical eyes during the 1870s and 1880s, and made vast, sweeping improvements in their standards. By the end of the century, doctors, lawyers, and teachers emerged from their schools with sound training behind them.

A Handful of Men Who Combined Depth and Perception

The great college presidents (*left to right*), Angell of Michigan, White of Cornell, McCosh of Princeton, and Eliot of Harvard, showed a remarkable combination of intellectual sagacity, administrative ability, and persuasive power. The liberal standards they set in their own institutions became guideposts for those creating new and mature universities.

It was only toward the end of the nineteenth century that extensive laboratory work and classroom demonstration became a major part of medical education in the United States. Here, the lecturer at the New York Polyclinic School of Medicine and Surgery has the floor.

SPORTS

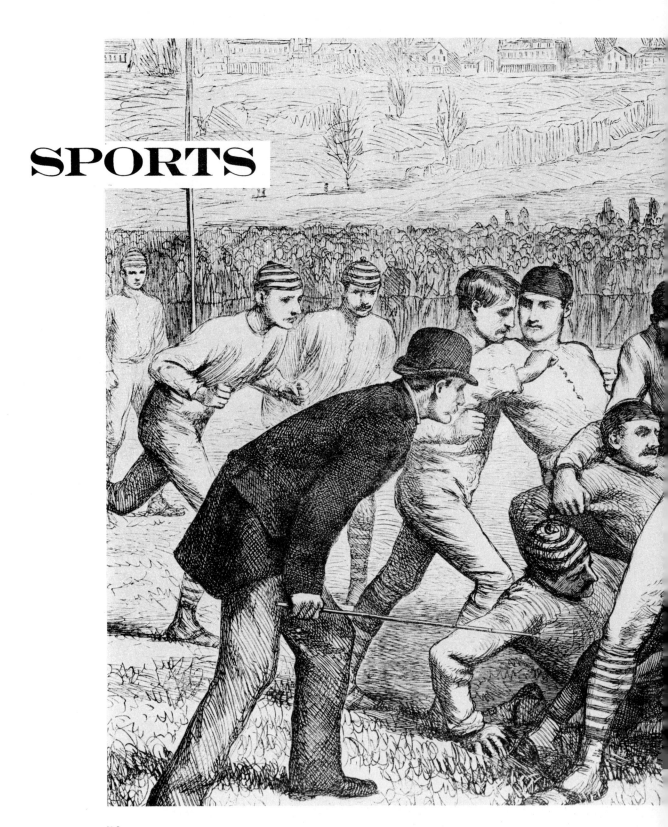

By the 1880s, Football and Baseball Reached Twin Peaks

THE BONE-CRUSHING operation pictured on pages 56-57, is a "football match" between Yale and Princeton in 1879. This strenuous sport, an offshoot of the English Rugby, was becoming a satisfying Roman spectacle on eastern campuses in the 1880s and 1890s. Lack of protective covering made the sport a bruising one but never put out the fires of undergraduate enthusiasm.

Walter Camp of Yale did much to give the game its present form; his ideas were responsible for the eleven-man team, the method of snapping the ball into play, and the system of tackling and interference. Before Camp's innovations, tackling below the waist was not permitted and the runner was dragged down by a multitude of arms around his neck.

When the more effective tackle was introduced, teams on the offense created flying wedges and circular formations to protect the ball carrier. Refinements of the rules broke up these beef trusts, put premiums on deception, and led to the open, tricky game of the twentieth century.

Football was for undergraduates. Baseball was for everybody. Of uncertain origins, the game was played before the Civil War but received great impetus during the conflict. Troops with idle time on their hands took to the game eagerly and a cross-fertilization occurred which caused the sport to spring up all over the United States in postbellum years.

The statement that Abner Doubleday invented the game has been strongly challenged. It is certain that he set down plans and procedures which did much to make baseball what it is today. The game evolved rapidly during the last decades of the century and by 1900 the basic regulations, still in use, were fixed.

The national game was an amateur affair in the beginning, and clubs arose in small towns as well as the larger cities. In their drive for top-quality players, the clubs began to violate amateur rules, subsidizing tricky pitchers and hard-hitting outfielders in a transparent fashion. Big sums were bet on

58

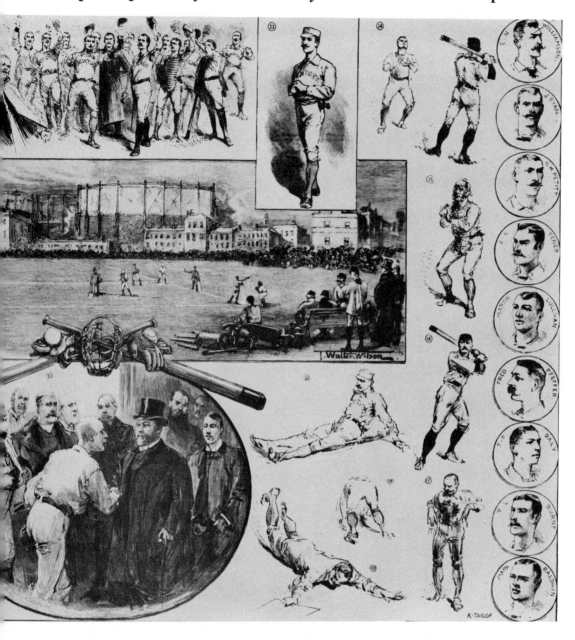

games and the temptation to bribery was strong.

The way out of the morass was the creation of outright professional teams. The Cincinnati Red Stockings led the way in 1869 and they were dynamite, playing an entire season without losing a single game. By 1876, the National League had been organized and the American League came just after the turn of the century.

Championship American teams sometimes toured Europe. In 1889, England saw Chicago vs. the All-Americans, and the Prince of Wales personally greeted the players (*above*).

Horse shows were utilitarian affairs, for the purpose of comparing the quality of animals bred for useful tasks, when they began in the United States. Gradually, competition for its own sake evolved. By the late 1890s, the New York Horse Show at Madison Square Garden was an important and glittering social function, and has continued as such.

A Crest in the Closing Decades of the Nineteenth Century

THE WORLD'S biggest democracy has always loved the sport of kings. American breeders had raced their horses since colonial days and the well-bred mounts of southern planters gave a decisive advantage to Confederate cavalry early in the Civil War. Just after the conflict, track followers could watch their favorites run in a series of gilded settings. Saratoga Springs and Jerome Park in New York were elegant, fashionable, and refined. New Jersey's commodious Monmouth Park (*above*) offered flat racing and the steeplechase. On a May day in 1875, the Kentucky Derby was inaugurated at Louisville and has remained a classic ever since.

The powerful American Jockey Club set the pattern for other such organizations which championed racing from coast to coast. Men of wealth, like Pierre Lorillard in the East and Leland Stanford in the West, established model stock farms to maintain the blood lines of their glossy-coated favorites.

Harness racing gave the masses the thrills flat racing induced in the classes. Pulling their fragile rigs, trotters and pacers were familiar sights at state fairs and on their own circuit tracks.

61

From the Golden Gate to Long Island Sound, There Was a Widespread Interest in Boats of All Types

IN THE days before the Civil War, an elegant American sailing vessel called *America* won a special trophy while sailing against the British in English waters. In the years which followed, the English made sporadic attempts to regain the *America's* cup with such ships as *Genesta* (*left, foreground*) but never achieved success. The international yacht race, whose challengers and defenders were built by syndicates of wealthy men, soon became an established tradition. Meanwhile, less wealthy Americans sailed dinghies, catboats, and other craft.

Rowing blossomed after the war, to become one of the nation's most vivid and colorful sports. Intercollegiate crew races dominated the picture at first, but private rowing clubs soon dotted the country. Of special interest was the "Schuylkill Navy," whose string of gingerbread boathouses lined the Philadelphia waterway's banks.

63

Though No Longer Needed for Subsistence, The Bow, Rifle,

I N A NATION so rich in game, it is no wonder that hunting and fishing persisted in nineteenth-century America. Weed-filled rivers flowing into the Atlantic were ideal for rail shooting (*far right*). Overhead, flocks of migrating mallards, teal, canvasback, and geese made inviting targets. The inland meadows abounded in grouse and quail.

Fishermen could troll for pickerel or pike in the Great Lakes, cast for bass or yellow perch, or watch trout rise in the cold-running streams. For the man who wanted size, tarpon flashed in the Gulf of Mexico (*lower right*).

Marksmen less inclined to killing joined the National Rifle Association. Outstanding shots entered international matches, such as that at Creedmore, Long Island, in 1876 (*below*).

Maid Marians found archery exciting (*right*); it also gave them a chance to modestly display their tiny waists and ample bosoms.

The Gentle Sports Brought Victorian Belles into the Open

SWAINS and their ladies basked in the eye of nature whenever possible as a relief from desk duties and the chores of housekeeping. The great outdoors fostered romance, and the picnic (*below*) provided a great opportunity for pairing off. Replete with food and drink, titillated by lawn games, young lovers could wander into the verdure, sail to islands in the nearby lake, or paddle their way into moonlight and romance.

Stay-at-homes were mad for croquet.

This pleasant pastime swept the nation on the heels of the Civil War. Wide, sun-flecked Victorian lawns made ideal settings for spirited matches. Equipment was imported from abroad, competitive teams organized, and a detailed code of rules established and sternly enforced. When torches were placed atop stakes for night play, young Lotharios found the situation ideal for wooing under the guise of sport.

Wooden balls, stakes, mallets, and

Air Which Tinted Their Cheeks and Warmed Their Blood

wickets accompanied many a picnic party. But the purists would have none of this, preferring to play on well-kept courses which had been scythed and clipped to perfection.

A change in the weather brought a brief interlude useful for hay rides; then the first protracted cold wave signaled the opening of the skating season.

The freeze-up of Philadelphia's rivers (*below*) brought out a dazzling crowd, bundled to the ears and flaunting every color of the rainbow. New York's Central Park was a haven for skaters; so were the thousands of natural and man-made lakes of the Midwest. Farm children explored the creeks and branches of their neighborhoods.

When everyone was out on a crisp winter day, moppets played tag and youths made the powdered ice fly in improvised hockey games. Young lovers crossed arms, skated in pairs. The more sedentary were tucked into sleighs.

Matching the craze for croquet was widespread enthusiasm for the bicycle, a somewhat dangerous vehicle boasting a front wheel five feet high. Bicycle club members, off on a week-end excursion, brought cheers from onlookers (*above*). Those who played it safer over Saturday and Sunday might cavort at beaches such as Long Branch, New Jersey (*below*).

Politics

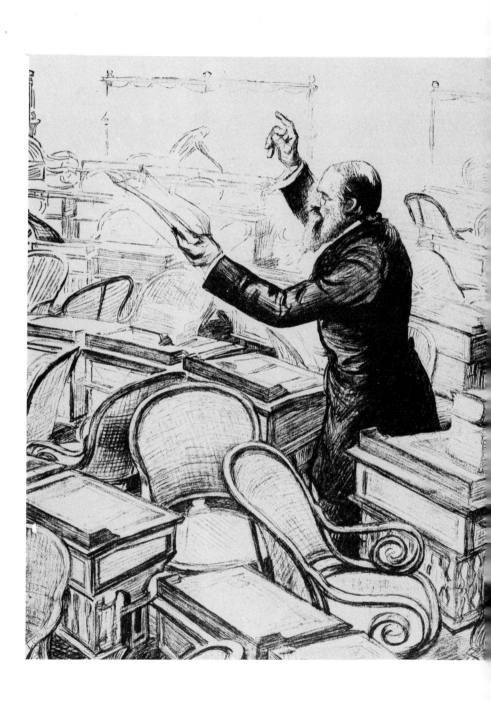

THE PRESIDENTS

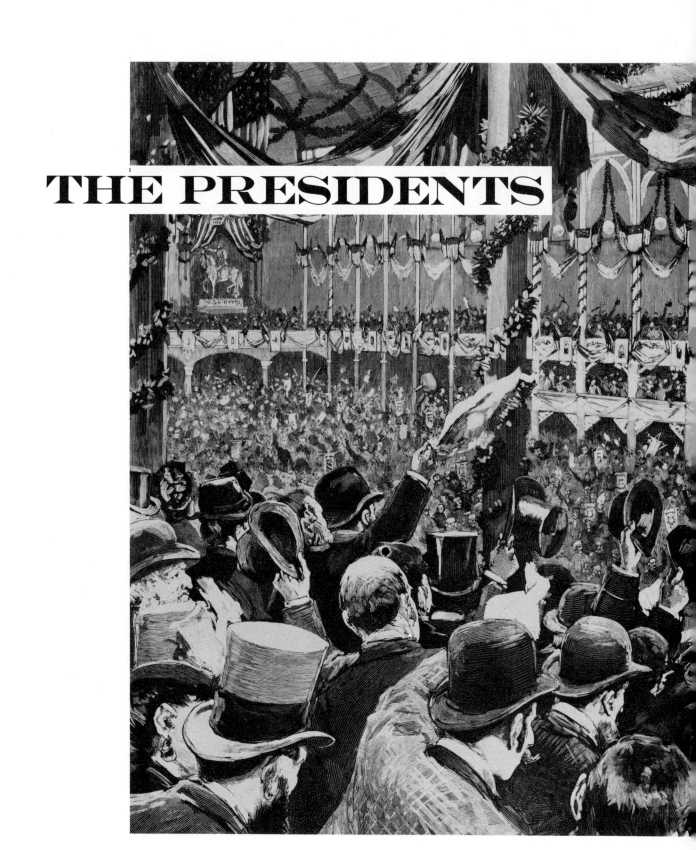

During the Election of 1868 the Presidency Fell
Like a Ripe Plum into the Hands of a Wartime Hero

WHEN impeachment proceedings failed to remove Andrew Johnson from office, the Radical Republicans had to await the will of the people. On May 20, 1868, the National Union Republican convention met in Chicago to select a presidential candidate and John Logan, a wartime comrade in arms, offered the name of Ulysses S. Grant (*above*). In a unanimous vote on the first ballot, the victor of Appomattox carried the day. Schuyler Colfax, Speaker of the House, was picked as Grant's running mate.

Bearing the Democratic banner was Horatio Seymour, governor of New York during the Civil War, with Francis P. Blair, Jr., of Missouri in the second position.

The basic issue of the campaign was Reconstruction. Defending their harsh methods in the "conquered provinces" the Radicals plumped for complete Negro suffrage in the South. Democratic speakers tore into the Radical record and denounced it.

The highest office in the land went to Grant, by an electoral count of 214 to eighty. Professional politicians, however, were disturbed by the popular vote which favored Grant by the slight margin of 53 per cent to 47 per cent. It was noted that the new President had lost New York and New Jersey. In addition, if the 650,000 Negro ballots in the South had not gone to Grant, he would not have had a majority of the popular vote. This was a danger signal to the Radicals, showing them the necessity of keeping carpetbag governments in office, and the importance of the Negro vote.

The new chief executive was a sore disappointment to the nation. Personally honest, he expected others to be the

Ulysses S. Grant

Schuyler Colfax

same and appeared to have no defense against the corrupt politicians, arrogant capitalists, and venal office seekers who surrounded him. Grant took advice freely, whether it was good or bad, and often acted on it to the detriment of his government. His cabinet appointments ranged from mediocre to poor, and his own personal aides used their powerful positions to private advantage. The President seemed awed by wealth and flattered by the attention of the rich.

It was an unfortunate period for a weak executive. In the North, the boom from the wartime years continued and the methods of free-wheeling big-money men called for investigation, if not regulation. The West was one vast ferment of Indian wars, railroad development, mining strikes, and emigrant arrivals. And all the evils of Reconstruction haunted the South.

Horatio Seymour took a middle-of-the-road position on Reconstruction but was lambasted by the northern press as an advocate of continued slavery and white supremacy.

Southern Problems Dominated Grant's First Term but There Was Ample Room for Scandal and Financial Panic

FRIGHTENED by the portents of the 1868 election, Radical Republicans pushed through the Fifteenth Amendment, with the help of southern states seeking to re-enter the Union, just before Grant took office. This amendment theoretically guaranteed the Negro's right to vote.

In practice, universal suffrage in the South was still a precarious privilege. Enraged by carpetbag governments and the rise of the Negro, the Ku Klux Klan and other night-riding societies carried out compaigns of calculated terror against former slaves, using murder and arson as their weapons. They got results.

Bitterly frustrated, both from the standpoint of idealism and political expediency, Congress replied with a series of three Enforcement Acts to trim the wings of the southerners. The first act, in May 1870, ordered heavy penalties for violations of the Fourteenth and Fifteenth Amendments. The second, in February 1871, sought to stamp out intimidation by placing state and congressional elections under U.S. government control. The third, also in 1871, was aimed at the Klan itself. It gave the President of the U.S.A. military privileges, including suspension of *habeas corpus*, to stamp out terrorism.

The acts were effective in proportion to their enforcement, which was rigid in many cases. By May 1872, Congress passed an Amnesty Act restoring the vote to a great number of former Confederates. Regaining their own suffrage, southerners ceased terrorism against

their former slaves and used more subtle pressures to drive them and their carpetbagger friends from the statehouses. By 1880, southern whites again were running their governments and voting solidly Democratic.

The results of the Civil War carried over into the field of international diplomacy. Grant's government came off well in this area, because of the work of one of his few first-class appointees, Secretary of State Hamilton Fish (*upper left*). At the Treaty of Washington in May 1871, the *Alabama* claims were submitted to international arbitration and the United States eventually received 15½ million dollars in damages for injuries to American shipping by British-built Confederate raiders during the war. The U.S. also reimbursed Great Britain for injuries done to her nationals and property as a result of the conflict.

Men of Fish's caliber were rare. Many of the President's associates were involved in shady deals. One was brought about by Jay Gould and James Fisk, a pair of scoundrels who sought to corner the market in gold and bid up its price. Grant was unwittingly involved, through the machinations of his relatives. The plot failed, but not before it brought "Black Friday" to the Gold Exchange (*left*) and wiped out a number of brokers.

Reaching deeper into the government was the scandal of the Crédit Mobilier, a company engaged in helping to build the Union Pacific Railway and making fat profits from contractors in the process. To prevent restrictive legislation, the company spread its stock (at cut-rate prices) among high-ranking members of the government. Those involved, investigation proved, included Vice-President Colfax, who retired in disgrace.

Disgusted by harsh Reconstruction measures and open scandals, a splinter group called the Liberal Republicans nominated Horace Greeley (*above*) to run against Grant in 1872. Democrats joined the procession but Greeley was soundly defeated by an electoral count of 286 to 66 and the nation prepared for four more years of "Grantism."

During the Course of Grant's Second Administration, The Nation Reached a New Low in Political Morality

THE POLITICAL chicanery of the first term was but a breath before the storm. As Grant kept faith with his followers and defended them, they stole the nation deaf, dumb, and blind.

Congress voted itself a 50 per cent salary increase, to be retroactive. The "Whisky Ring" was exposed as a combination of internal revenue officers and distillers formed to cheat the government out of its liquor taxes. War Secretary William W. Belknap resigned to avoid impeachment for accepting bribes from an Indian Agent over a period of years.

During the time of Grant, the nation's leading city festered in the same kind of evil. "Boss" William M. Tweed of Tammany Hall had an iron grip on New York City politics. He used his power to rob the taxpayers, through fraudu-

lent contracts and heavily padded bills submitted by contractors who were in on crooked deals, to the tune of millions of dollars. Diligent spadework by the *New York Times* and the vitriolic cartoons of Thomas Nast in *Harper's Weekly* helped bring the culprits to justice and Tweed was sentenced to prison by an aroused citizenry. The Nast cartoon "Let Us Prey" (*right*) showing Tweed surrounded by his henchmen as the lightning of indignation strikes might have stood for affairs in Washington as well as New York.

Grant, above and beyond corruption, had further fires heaped on his head as the nation faced a severe panic in 1873. The great banking house of Jay Cooke and Company closed its doors and repercussions were felt as far as the money markets of San Francisco (*below*).

76

Tilden (*right*) had done his best to stay unembroiled during the Civil War but Hayes (*left*) served the Union and was a brevet major general. Such a record was a sure bid for the vote of the boys in blue (*below*) who were organized as the Grand Army of the Republic, a veterans' organization whose parades and barbecues added up to power.

Picked to Succeed Grant and Clean Up the Mess in Washington, Hayes Entered Office Under a Cloud

RUTHERFORD B. HAYES was not one of our more glamorous presidents. But he was personally honest, hard-working, courageous, and a man of pristine ideals who had served three terms as governor of Ohio. It was his great misfortune to assume the highest office in the land under suspicious circumstances.

Made the Republican standard bearer on the seventh ballot at the convention, Hayes ran against Democrat Samuel J. Tilden who, as governor of New York, had helped smash the Tweed Ring.

Republican corruption and the continuing strains of Reconstruction were major campaign issues. When the returns poured in, Tilden had 51 per cent of the popular vote and 184 electoral votes, one short of the necessary majority. Hayes had 165 electoral votes. Twenty votes were in doubt, one from Oregon and the rest from southern states. The key electoral votes came from Louisiana, South Carolina and Florida where Radical Republican governments and local Democratic southerners were in deadly battle.

Because of claims and counterclaims, Congress appointed a special commission of fifteen to decide on the electoral vote issue. After many meetings (*below*), the decision was made on strict party lines and Hayes assumed office. It was the closest election in American history.

79

HARPER'S WEEKLY.

JOURNAL OF CIVILIZATION.

Vol. XXI.—No. 1056.]   NEW YORK, SATURDAY, MARCH 24, 1877.   [WITH A SUPPLEMENT. PRICE TEN CENTS.

Entered according to Act of Congress, in the Year 1877, by Harper & Brothers, in the Office of the Librarian of Congress, at Washington.

OUR NEW PRESIDENT—TAKING THE OATH.—Drawn by I. P. Pranishnikoff from a Photograph by Brady.—[See Page 230.]

There Was Much to Be Done in Washington and Hayes Made a Solid Contribution During His Years in Office

A**T THE** time of Hayes's inauguration, *Harper's Weekly* accurately predicted the contest which would begin the administration: "It is a contest provoked and led by the men whose leadership has brought the party to which they profess peculiar devotion into imminent peril. It is a leadership which would foster sectional hate as political capital, and which depends on the bribery of the Civil Service as the basis of party organization."

The influential publication had guessed the route the new President would follow. High on his agenda were restoration of peace and good government to the South, and civil service reform. The new broom was to sweep clean, and Hayes's cabinet appointments made old-time Republicans wince. The Postmaster General, David M. Key, was a Tilden Democrat, and a southern one to boot. Carl Schurz, Secretary of the Interior, was a European-born busybody with the flame of reform in his eyes.

Hayes began his term by ordering Federal troops, who were sustaining Republican governments, out of South Carolina and Louisiana. The Democrats immediately took over the governments. In January 1877, a Democratic governor took office in Florida.

"He serves his party best who serves his country best," Hayes had said during the campaign. Such a statement smacked of the goody-goody and was rank heresy to old-line entrenched politicians luxuriating in the spoils system so often attacked by the acid pen of Thomas Nast (*above, right*).

The zealous President violently opposed assessments on officeholders by political machines for the party fund; helped Schurz establish a merit system in Interior; and brought about sweep-

ing reforms in the postal and customs systems.

Money matters bulked large in Hayes's administration. The Civil War had been financed largely by greenbacks, paper money backed only by the government's promise to pay. Under Hayes, and because of the Resumption Act of 1875, greenbacks were made redeemable at full face value in gold. The newly formed Greenback party continued to plump for cheap, fiat money but eventually swung over to the "free silver" men who pushed through the Bland-Allison Act in 1878, authorizing the Treasury to purchase between 2 million and 4 million dollars' worth of silver each month and coin it as silver currency.

THE REPUBLICAN Party was split into two camps, the "Stalwarts," or tough-minded practical politicians, and the "Half-Breeds," made up of gentler souls like Hayes and James G. Blaine. At the Chicago convention in 1880 (*below*), the Stalwarts called for Grant again while the Half-Breeds favored Blaine. The going was hot and heavy and not until the thirty-sixth ballot was a compromise pounded out: James A. Garfield, backed by the Half-Breeds, for President, with Stalwart Chester A. Arthur in the second position.

Tired of being smeared as the party of treason, the Democrats nominated a Civil War general, Winfield S. Hancock, the hero of Gettysburg.

There were no campaign issues to speak of. Reconstruction was over and the nation was rolling in prosperity. Garfield slipped gently into office by an electoral vote of 214 to 155 although the candidates shared the popular vote almost equally.

Garfield was part of the schoolbook tradition. Born in a log cabin, he was a farmer, lay preacher, and a student at Williams.

By the Time of the 1880 Presidential Election, U.S. Politics Was in the Doldrums for Lack of Issues

Hancock was popular around the country, and cartoonists pictured him in the act of transferring new blood into the Democratic Party. His personality had little to do with his defeat, which was the result of much general inertia and apathy among the population.

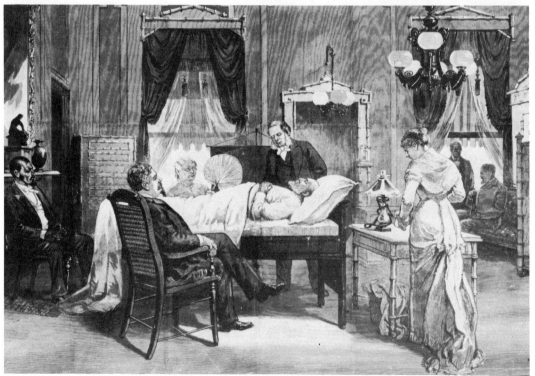

84

Cut Down by an Assassin's Gun, Garfield Yielded His High Office to a Member of the Stalwart Faction

PRESIDENT GARFIELD'S potential as chief executive will remain forever unknown. Shortly after the inauguration, a disappointed office seeker named Charles J. Guiteau pumped two bullets into the President's back at the Washington railroad station in the presence of Secretary of State Blaine (*upper left*). Given the best of care, the injured man lingered on for some time (*left*) but finally succumbed at Elberon, New Jersey, on September 19, 1881. Guiteau was arrested, tried, and hanged for the crime.

Elevation of Arthur (*above*) to the presidential seat created a watchful uneasiness in the country. Chester Alan Arthur was rich, a socialite, a Stalwart, and considered by many a political hack who had never held back from using the spoils system in New York state. There was immense gratification and surprise as Arthur let it be known he was his own man, creating a strong personal administration.

Despite his own shady past, Arthur attacked the spoils system and carried on Hayes's attempts at civil service reform. Pointing up the need for incorruptible men in high places were the "Star Route" frauds in which contractors cheated and lied about delivery of mail in the West, grossing money they had not earned and spreading a part of the graft among government officials.

In 1882, the nation sent a Democratic majority to the House and the Republicans sat up, looked around, and decided this was a manifesto calling for a civil service program, among other things. By the Pendleton Act, Congress acceded to Arthur's call for a decent civil service and directed that he form a bipartisan Civil Service Commission of three men to establish a merit system and set up competitive examinations. More than fifteen thousand government jobs were affected and although this was only a drop in the bucket, it was a firm advance which was later immensely improved.

High tariffs and other revenue producers left the government with an embarrassment of riches and congressmen reached into the pork barrel for appropriations to benefit their own constituents. Arthur vetoed an 18-million-dollar rivers-and-harbors bill of this type, but it passed over his veto.

Pumping money into the treasury, the tariff was rapidly becoming a political factor of importance. An attempt at reform was made during Arthur's administration but it had little value or effect. There was firm legislation on immigration in a bill excluding Chinese laborers for ten years, in response to demands from the West.

During the Presidential Campaign of 1884, Both Sides Thoroughly Indulged in Savage, Bitter Vituperation

I N 1884 a sizzling campaign for the presidency brought the nation out of tne political doldrums and made every man a partisan. Both parties split down the middle and the machine-supported candidate was defeated by a tough, vigorous independent.

Carrying the Republican banner was James G. Blaine of Maine, dubbed the "Plumed Knight" in a surge of dubious rhetoric. Secretary of State under Garfield, Blaine itched for the highest office and had been passed over in previous nominations.

Blaine (*upper right*) carried certain political liabilities in the form of unsavory deeds while in office and thus alienated the "Mugwumps," a group of liberal, reform-minded Republicans. But the man had tremendous magnetism and carried the convention on the fourth ballot. Educator E. B. Andrews described the scene: "The announcement of Blaine's nomination unleashed the

latent insanity of ten thousand people within the hall. Hats were thrown high in air, umbrellas whirled around, the State shields torn down and borne proudly upon filial breasts."

The Democrats put up a powerful candidate in Grover Cleveland (*upper left*), the "Veto Mayor" of Buffalo and a reform governor of New York state. Big, hard, honest, self-reliant, Cleveland plowed his own furrow without Tammany help and caught the public imagination.

The Mugwumps supported Cleveland, as did many Catholics, alienated by a slighting Republican reference. New York was the key state and Cleveland managed to swing it. Tense crowds braved the rain in New York City's Printing House Square (*right*) to watch the close figures being posted. In the end, Cleveland garnered 219 electoral votes to 182 for Blaine, although his popular majority was tiny.

A Happy Wedding Brought Joy to the Nation After Its Day

GROVER CLEVELAND was the sturdy symbol of Victorian man, bluff and straight-speaking. He liked steak for breakfast and it showed on his ample build. The heavy-set bachelor delighted the nation when he succumbed to romance and became the first President to be married in the White House.

Cleveland's bride was young Frances Folsom, who had been his ward after the death of her father in 1875. The presidential mansion was turned into a flower-bedecked palace for the wedding, which took place June 2, 1886, in the Blue Room (*above*). Miss Folsom carried no flowers and wore no jewels except her engagement ring of sapphires and diamonds. The Marine Band, in scarlet and gold, played "Mendelssohn's Wedding March" and all but one of the Cabinet attended. The honeymoon cottage was at Deer Park, Maryland. Among the couple's presents was a gold smelling-salts bottle set with diamonds.

A year before his wedding, Cleveland sent a sympathetic letter to Julia Grant on the death of her husband. Ulysses S. Grant had followed the presidency with a triumphal world tour, then returned to New York to enter the banking business. The venture failed badly and the family was in financial straits. In 1884, Grant contracted cancer of the throat. In pain and sorrow, he worked on his memoirs to keep poverty from his kin when death should overtake him.

When the disease took his voice, the Silent Man, as he was called, became a symbol of suffering courage to the people. At his death, in July, 1885, his presidential sins were forgiven and America mourned the hero of the western and Virginia campaigns. He was buried on a bank of the Hudson, as artillery echoed from the rocky walls of the Palisades.

Of Mourning for the Passing of a Brave National Hero

Groups of prominent physicians attended the ailing general in his last days but there was no way of arresting the killing disease. Grant died at Mount McGregor, near Saratoga, New York. Prominent Confederate generals like Joseph E. Johnston came to his funeral.

IN 1886, the United States Senate (*above*) had seventy-six members and was "the club" which functioned in a manner rich in dignity and propriety. There were 325 members in the House of Representatives (*right*), every one of whom "has an indefinite number of bills and at least one great speech to deliver," according to a contemporary reporter.

Government of the United States lay in the hands of these men, and they had been accustomed to rule ever since their predecessors had trimmed down the executive power wielded by Lincoln and Johnson. Congressmen watched with something of a shock as President Cleveland set about negating their decisions.

The chief executive vetoed 310 bills after taking office—more than all the other presidents combined—and elimi-

nated over a hundred more by pocket veto. Cleveland was a man not averse to using the clenched fist. When he felt something ought not to be, he said so, with a supreme disregard of where the chips fell.

Clamoring for increased pensions, on the flimsiest of trumped-up excuses, veterans rode their Congressmen hard and over four thousand pension bills passed during Cleveland's tenure. He examined them with care, vetoing many and earning the permanent enmity of the former soldiers.

Another faction angered by Cleveland's principles was that segment of big business which was under the protection of high-tariff laws. From tariffs and internal revenue, the government coffers were bursting with an annual surplus of about 100 million dollars.

90

Cleveland Was the Strongest Chief Executive Since Lincoln but He Had to Battle a Divided Congress

To reduce this embarrassing amount and free the money for circulation, the President called for tariff reductions. The so-called "protected industries" were no longer in need of a high-tariff wall, and the chief executive argued that lower rates would bring financial benefits to all the American people. Cleveland could not bring the House and Senate into agreement on his tariff proposals but the issue was an explosive one in the next presidential campaign.

Big business was involved in an additional way during Cleveland's administration, this time by the actions of Congress in relation to operation of railroads in the United States. The rail lines had mushroomed and their operators joined together to milk the public. This was done by fraudulent capitalization and stock watering, by "pools" or mo-

nopolies to control large shares of business, and by rebates and rate discrimination.

State control of railroad rates had been declared unconstitutional despite the fight put up by embattled farmers who had fought for local legislation. In 1885, the Senate appointed a special committee headed by Senator Shelby M. Cullom of Illinois and as a result of the committee's work, the Interstate Commerce Act came into being in 1887.

The act forbade special rates and secret rebates as well as unfair discrimination, killed pooling agreements, and gave the public the right to inspect rates and schedules. It was a pioneer piece of legislation in declaring that the government had a right to regulate private industry when public interest was involved.

Republican Politicians Picked a New Man to Battle With Cleveland in 1888 and Emerged from the Fray Victorious

WHEN the Democrats met in convention at St. Louis on June 5, 1888, there was little doubt as to their choice. Insurgents and Tammany politicians agreed and incumbent Grover Cleveland was picked by acclamation (pages 70-71) to make the presidential race again. No other candidate was mentioned. As his running mate, the President had Allen G. Thurman of Ohio.

Republicans fished in muddier waters, for Blaine, the Plumed Knight, had indicated he would refuse the nomination. Votes were split among a handful of men until the eighth ballot when the convention picked Benjamin Harrison of Indiana, a man as pure as a mountain stream and equally colorless. To make sure of the eastern vote, the Republicans picked Levi P. Morton of New York for the vice-presidential position.

Harrison (*upper right*) was the grandson of William Henry Harrison, ninth President of the United States. Benjamin Harrison studied and practiced law, and served in the Civil War in which he was made a brevet brigadier general. He served from 1881 to 1887 in the United States Senate.

Both Harrison and Cleveland had records of honesty and sincerity in public affairs but beyond this shared virtue, they differed widely. Cleveland was warm, open, friendly, and powerful; Harrison somewhat cold in his personal relationships and gave no demonstration of force or indignation. The campaign, however, did not revolve around personalities.

Money greased wheels in the 1888 presidential race and there was only one major issue: the tariff. Cleveland's forthright demand for tariff cuts had

split the protection issue along party lines. The Democrats became defenders of tariff reduction, the Republicans sought to maintain high-duty walls.

The tariff issue was a powerful lever as used by Republican leaders who announced that any lowering of duties would encourage the flooding of American markets with cheap foreign goods, eventually driving down the wages and standard of living of American workingmen. With this plea for the popular vote in the air, party workers turned to powerful businessmen protected by tariff laws and demanded money for their war chests. The manufacturers gave freely to protect their own price structure. The money was used to form Republican clubs by thousands.

The machinery worked well; Harrison carried the uncertain states of New York and Indiana and gained office by an electoral count of 233 to 168. Cleveland had a popular plurality of a hundred thousand votes.

92

VOL. 15 NO. 385   MARCH 2 1889.   PRICE 10 CENTS.

ENTERED AT THE POST OFFICE AT NEW YORK AS SECOND-CLASS MATTER.   COPYRIGHT 1889 BY THE JUDGE PUBLISHING CO..

OUT AND IN.

GROVER.—I am driven from home, and I'm sadly forlorn:
I don't know just where I shall go.
The landlord got tired of *promise*, and said
I was English—too English, you know.

BENJAMIN.—I think I can manage to fill the White House
With some *bric-a-brac* not at all slow;
An Administration with sand in its heart,
That is Yankee—quite Yankee, you know.

A *Judge* editorial gave thanks for freedom from "four years of Democratic purgatory," while a cartoon made Harrison a hero in Yankee Doodle clothes. Cleveland's stand on the tariff, and his backing by the British minister at Washington, made him a target as a "free trader" who favored European workingmen at the expense of those of the U.S.A.

TARIFFS, trusts, and tillers of the soil held the spotlight during Harrison's administration, which was a busy one.

The President himself showed no great vigor in office. Better known to the public were Secretary of State James G. Blaine, extremely active in foreign affairs; Thomas B. Reed of Maine, Speaker of the House and "czar" of that body by reason of his iron control; and William McKinley of Ohio, Chairman of the House Ways and Means Committee.

It fell to the latter gentleman to provide a new tariff bill, in response to Republican campaign pledges. McKinley's tariff, put into effect after a certain amount of study, debate, and horse trading in the halls of Congress, set the highest duties on manufactured goods in American history. The protective tariff was sacred to McKinley and the new bill gave it full sway. Tariff rates on metal products and textiles were increased; the principle of protection was extended to farm produce; articles not competing with American products were put on the free list; and reciprocity agreements were authorized.

As the price for passing the tariff, western interests had called for unlimited coinage of free silver. They did not get their way completely, but the Sherman Silver Purchase Act of 1890 was a compromise which said the government would purchase $4\frac{1}{2}$ million ounces of silver each month and issue treasury certificates, redeemable in gold or silver, against the purchased metal.

In the meantime, manufacturers and middlemen began to raise prices, a move made possible by the high-tariff walls. The capitalists were delighted; the consumers groaned and protested. And their protests were aimed not only at the tariff-caused prices in particular, but at the structure of American capitalism in general.

Size was catching up with America and was forcing a reassessment of the old ways of doing things. The nation had always been pledged to a laissez-faire economy, with the government keeping its hands off private business operations. But the benign attitude no longer suited the facts.

There was a growing trend toward economic consolidation. The competition which was supposed to regulate prices under a laissez-faire economy was disappearing. Increasing trends toward monopoly in important industries meant concentrations of power, elimination of competition, and destruction of the small manufacturer and businessman. There were possible economic advantages to these new, huge trusts and holding companies, but in the 1880s they appeared to be snowed under by the evils of combination. These were increased prices, control of natural resources by private combines, and the power of big business to influence legislation.

States had tried to regulate monopoly with little success. Senate investigations showed it was the national government's turn, and in 1890 the Sherman Antitrust Act was passed, declaring trusts and combinations in restraint of trade to be illegal. Because it dealt only with trade and not manufacturing, the act was loose and ineffective. But it served notice to the controllers of industry and business that the government would try to protect the public interest, as it had in 1887 with the Interstate Commerce Commission.

The Sherman Act was one symptom of the feeling of revolt which swept many of the common people during the 1880s. Perhaps the biggest single seg-

The People Who Were Against Business Consolidation

ment of the population up in arms was the group which operated the farms. In 1867, the Patrons of Husbandry, or the Grange, had been founded and a few years later it was fighting for the Granger Laws to stem railroad abuses. The Greenback party drew farm support. Later, the National Farmer's Alliance (representing the Northwest) and the Farmer's Alliance and Industrial Union (representing the South) called for justice to the farmer, who was represented as a victim (*below*) who paid outmoded internal revenue measures called "war taxes," while the monopolists gathered in the milk brought them under their high-tariff policies.

In the 1880s, the farmers had much to be bitter about: overproduction in some areas, dropping prices, and drought.

Further organization, to get political power, appeared to be the answer. Labor groups were invited to join, and in 1891-92, the People's Party of the United States of America was hammered out of the "Populist" movement. It was formally organized in February 1892, and a few months later laid down a stinging manifesto to the nation calling for an income tax, free-silver coinage, government ownership of utilities, restriction of immigration, the eight-hour day, and other pertinent reforms.

A New Voice in Politics Lent Spice to the Otherwise Mundane Presidential Campaign of 1892

THE PEOPLE'S PARTY, generally called "Populist," was on the march and in the presidential campaign of 1892 they put up James B. Weaver of Iowa for President and former Rebel James G. Field of Virginia for Vice-President.

Either free and unlimited coinage of silver at a ratio of sixteen to one with gold, or issue of paper money, appealed to Populist thinking. The farmer apparently wanted to pay his debts in cheap money, with little thought of the ruinous effects a major inflation might have on the nation.

Blaine tried for the Republican nomination, resigning as Secretary of State just before the time for decision came at the convention, but the delegates settled once again for the glamorless Harrison. He got the nomination on the first ballot, and Whitelaw Reid of the New York *Tribune* was given second position.

Working behind his back and without his knowledge, Democrats pushed hard for Grover Cleveland, with success.

Adlai E. Stevenson of Illinois was the choice for Vice-President.

Republicans carried a heavy series of burdens to the polls. The McKinley tariff had raised prices. Cleveland's courageous stand on pensions had been reversed and Harrison's signing of the Dependent Pension Bill helped increase pension appropriations from 89 million to 159 million dollars in four years. As to civil service reform, Harrison had acted badly and even appointed his own relatives to the government payroll. There had been an attempt to force Federal supervision of elections in the South. And the Sherman Antitrust Act had proved too weak to be effective.

Cleveland swept the election, with 277 electoral votes to Harrison's 145, and 46 per cent of the popular vote to 43 per cent for his rival. The Populists made news as their party's candidate pulled twenty-two electoral votes and more than a million ballots from the people. Politicians looked up at the show of People's Party strength.

Facing a cheering crowd at New York's Madison Square Garden (*above*), Cleveland was given official notice of his victory at the convention. The President was beginning to show his age, but his wife appeared as winsome as ever (*lower left*). Stevenson (*below*), a successful lawyer, served the Post Office Department during Cleveland's first administration.

The White House Was No Bed of Roses for Cleveland the

The Panic of 1893 sent a series of flurries through the New York Stock Exchange and bidding on the floor often became frenzied as investors unloaded. While depression spread, four hundred banks, including nineteen national ones, closed their doors to the public.

CLEVELAND'S second term put the President through a wringer. He had to face financial panic, a costly nationwide strike, a tariff with which he disagreed wholeheartedly, and growing dissension in his own party.

The opulent eighties were over and so was the "billion-dollar Congress" whose lavish spending, Speaker Thomas B. Reed had said, was appropriate for a "billion-dollar country." Government credit was somewhat shaken by the steady depletion of the gold reserve. Reduction in revenue and pouring out of money for pensions was drying up the surpluses of the past.

It had been the custom of the Treasury to maintain a gold reserve of 100 million dollars to meet its obligations, and because that metal reserve was

known to exist, people did not turn in their paper money to be redeemed in gold. But by terms of the Sherman Silver Purchase Act, the government took in 54 million ounces of silver annually, issuing paper redeemable in either gold or silver against it. Gold was the preferred metal; as the citizens saw the continuing flood of paper being issued, they brought it in for redemption. As Cleveland took office, the gold reserve was shrinking steadily.

Action by the President finally ended the Silver Purchase Act on November 1, 1893, which brought some relief. But gold reserves continued to shrink as foreign creditors called for payment in the yellow metal and foreign holders of American investments dumped them in this country, taking payment in gold.

98

Second Time Around as His Party Was Often Against Him

Cleveland issued bonds to bring in gold and eventually made a deal with a powerful banking syndicate in 1895 through which the financial partners bought government bonds in exchange for gold, then sold them at high profit to themselves. The President was criticized for "selling out to Wall Street," but government credit was saved.

The fears over gold, along with factors such as overexpansion in industry, agricultural hardships, and financial troubles abroad, brought on the Panic of 1893. Businesses failed in alarming numbers, unemployment shot up, and the dark clouds of depression came down over the land.

Adding to the general misery was a long and costly railroad strike which began at the Pullman Company in Illinois and gradually became a nationwide battle between railroad management and the American Railway Union. The country was paralyzed, and both bayonets and injunctions were used to restore normal service (page 187).

Further headaches came when the President called for tariff revision putting iron, timber, coal, wool, and sugar on the free list and requesting an income tax. When the ragged bill finally passed, it carried 634 amendments. The income tax provision was declared unconstitutional by the Supreme Court.

Spotlighting the depression was a march of the unemployed on Washington led by "General" Jacob Coxey of Ohio. The leader, who demanded a public works program and a big issue of paper money, was arrested for walking on the broad White House lawn.

99

Mr. Hanna's Stand on the Labor Question.

PRE-ELECTION campaigning in 1896 was a classic example of back-room politics. Dominating these hideaways for the Republicans was Marcus A. Hanna (*above, with fan*) of Cleveland, a wealthy politician dedicated to making Governor William McKinley of Ohio President of the United States.

McKinley, best known for his high-tariff leanings, was an affable, courteous gentleman of no great color who campaigned from his front porch at Canton. Republicans, in the face of a surge of interest in free coinage of silver and a bimetallic system, boldly declared against such proposals and endorsed a single gold standard, high tariffs, liberal pensions for veterans, and compulsory arbitration of labor disputes when interstate commerce was affected.

The opposition took a dim view of Hanna's stand on labor (*right*).

100

West to Dramatize the 1896 Presidential Campaign

FOR SHEER political glamour, William Jennings Bryan of Nebraska (*right*) was to McKinley as the sun is to the moon. Handsome, florid, a master of emotion, the young man smothered his listeners in floods of orotund oratory. He had been lawyer, Congressman, and newspaper editor but was best known for his defense of free silver.

Unlimited coinage of gold and silver, at a ratio of sixteen to one, was the major issue of the campaign. Bimetallism had become the panacea for the ills of the farmer and the workingman.

Advocates of free silver caucused throughout the land (*below*) and found their biggest support in the West and South. Democrats in these areas were fiery advocates of free silver, as were the Populists who had made soft money their own cause. Eastern Democrats and some of those in the Midwest remained hard-money men.

Sharp Rift Between Republicans and Democrats

MARK HANNA'S well-oiled machine worked smoothly when the Republicans met at St. Louis in June (*left*), and McKinley (*right*) was nominated on the first ballot.

Shortly afterward, the Democrats met at Chicago (*lower left*) in a tumultuous convention punctuated by Indian war whoops, fist fights, and waterfalls of words. Free-silver men hacked away at the men representing eastern interests and the supporters of Cleveland. The Democrat party had gradually become the refuge of the workingman and the farmer who opposed eastern capitalist control of bank loans, mortgages, and the means of industrial production. It was to these men that Bryan spoke as he unleashed his impressive voice in a plea for free silver, ending with an impassioned outburst:

"Having behind us the producing masses of this nation and the world, supported by the commercial interests, the laboring interests, and the toilers everywhere, we will answer their demand for a gold standard by saying to them: 'You shall not press down upon the brow of labor this crown of thorns—you shall not crucify mankind upon a cross of gold.'"

The warm words worked well for Bryan and he received the nomination upon the fifth ballot. With the Democrats in the hands of free silverites, the Populists had little choice but to go along, and they declared for Bryan.

Bryan barnstormed the country, making speech after speech on the silver issue and turning on his personal charm. McKinley stayed home but Hanna spent money freely on propaganda. It did the trick, and McKinley won the election by an electoral vote of 271 to 176. The East and Midwest were solid for McKinley, as were California and Oregon.

THE ILLUSTRATED LONDON NEWS.

REGISTERED AT THE GENERAL POST OFFICE AS A NEWSPAPER.

No. 3004.—VOL. CIX.   SATURDAY, NOVEMBER 7, 1896.   TWO WHOLE SHEETS! SIXPENCE. By Post, 6½d.

THE NEW PRESIDENT OF THE UNITED STATES, MAJOR WILLIAM McKINLEY.

The Depression Vanished with McKinley's Election
And the Entire Nation Prepared to Make Money

The most spectacular avowal of the United States' new interest in world affairs was the war with Spain, one immediate cause of which was the sinking of the *Maine* (*above*) in Cuban coastal waters. Whether the explosion which sank the light battleship was an accident or deliberate was never determined but "Remember the *Maine!*" made a fine slogan.

TIMES were booming as McKinley led the nation, and Congress nailed down an election plank with the Gold Standard Act, declaring the gold dollar to be the unit of value in the United States. The tariff came in for a thorough going-over and the Dingley Bill which resulted had the highest tariff rates in U.S. history.

As the country prospered, the United States took a new, giant step forward, entering the world of foreign affairs in earnest. A war with Spain which lasted less than three months (pages 293-303) enriched the U.S.A. with new territory: Guam, Puerto Rico, and the Philippine Islands. In the same decade, Hawaii was annexed.

Andrew D. White, U.S. ambassador to Berlin, took a strong part in the Hague Conference of 1899 calling for arbitration of grievances between nations.

Citizens of the Hawaiian Islands demonstrated joyously as news of their annexation by the United States was announced in 1898.

Town and Country

THE CITIES

The catfish woman.

"T HEY ... deem it a necessary condition of human improvement that
towns should abound," said John Stuart
Mill as he spoke of the Americans.

Whether or not nineteenth-century
citizens of the U.S.A. deemed it necessary, there did occur a fantastic rise in
the number and population of the cities,
from 1865 to 1900. By 1890, one-third
of the nation lived in towns, and
farmers and immigrants were helping
swell the totals yearly.

In the Midwest, so rapid was the
growth rate that the cities closely re-
sembled one another, carved as they
were from the prairies and flatlands.
Eastern commonwealths, polished with
age, retained their distinctive character despite their own population in-
creases.

Philadelphia's Chestnut Street (*left*)

Century America Was the Enormous City Growth

was dark, narrow, and old-fashioned, with horsecar tracks and buildings which rose to the decorous height of six stories. In the residential sections, as well as downtown, street carriers still went their rounds (*left and below*) in 1892.

The Quaker City was placid, peaceful, and serene, as its founders had planned it. Washed by the Delaware and Schuylkill Rivers, Philadelphia dozed in the sun after a meal of pepper pot soup, fat capon, and magnificent local ice cream. From 1870 to 1890, the population increased by more than a quarter million.

Boston was a dowager of a city, respected and venerable, where the policeman at the corner of State and Washington paused to chat with beshawled old ladies (*right*). Twisting cobblestoned streets, an inordinate love of the inhabitants for brown bread and codfish cakes, and a stern respect for the New England intellect were part of the Boston tradition. A flood of Irish immigration pushed the city toward the half-million mark in the 1890s.

110

Washington Did Not Approach Other Major Cities in Size but Its Pace Quickened as the Century Ended

A T THE close of the Civil War, Washington was an easygoing city with time for summer concerts on the Capitol grounds (*far left*) and the worst-paved streets of any major capital. By the 1890s, miles of asphalt were withstanding snowstorms and sustaining heavy traffic (*lower left*) as the city passed the quarter-million mark.

Swelling the population were professional lobbyists (*left*), representing special interests, who poured out money freely.

To the north lay Baltimore (*below*), more social and more gentle than the capital. The city was booming commercially and *Scribner's* called it the "Liverpool of America" in 1894, but it remained the abode of southern gentlemen who took time from their countinghouses to sample soft-shell crabs and canvasback duck in season.

Manhattan Was the Pride of the Nation but Its Inhabitants Were Too Busy to Boast of Its Charms

NEW YORK was the magnet which drew visitors from abroad and the hinterlands alike. The pride of the city, and her shame, lay in the streets. Downtown Broadway (*left*) held a hurly-burly of human beings, each wanting to be somewhere else. In early morning, at lunch time, and in the evening, traffic became a solid blockade.

A May morning on Fifth Avenue at the Plaza, just below Central Park, showed a peace and grandeur rivaling that of any Paris boulevard (*below*). Nursemaids wheeled their umbrella-protected tots, ladies rode sidesaddle, and all glowed warmly in the sunshine.

The great city had everything for everybody. Restless, vital, everchanging, it was the place to see and be seen. There were 1½ million people in New York in 1890, and eight hundred thousand more in Brooklyn, a separate city. Not until 1898 was Greater New York, made up of five boroughs, created.

A BEAUTIFUL YOUNG WIDOW'S NARROW ESCAPE.
ALLEGED BRUTAL ATTEMPT TO RAVISH MRS. SUSAN ESTERLY, NEAR ELIZABETH, NEW JERSEY.

The Police Gazette Lovingly Chronicled Them All

VISITORS to New York, in the years between the Civil War and the turn of the century, found a group of palatial hotels waiting for their custom. Among the older ones were the St. Nicholas, the Clarendon, the Park Avenue, and the Murray Hill, and the last decade of the century saw the Waldorf-Astoria and the Plaza come into being. Delmonico's and other gilded restaurants offered the finest in game and seafood. A guest of the city, from Paris or London, might dine as he pleased after a day in the countinghouses of Wall Street, then choose ballet, opera, or a legitimate play for his evening's entertainment. If he wished to stake a fortune on the turn of a card, he could be accommodated in luxurious surroundings.

A man of more mundane taste found the beer gardens to his liking, and the concert saloons, featuring dancing girls with music. If he should crave headier wine, a procession of pimps, prostitutes, petty gamblers, and bunco steerers existed to separate him from his money.

Vice was a big and sprawling industry during the Mauve Decade in Manhattan and like any major industry, it had a historian, in the *Police Gazette*. The lively publication kept a watchful eye on the more lurid crimes of the city and the outlying districts, reporting them in stories rich with detail. Boxing, wrestling, and horse-playing received their due in the pink pages of the magazine, which also did a tidy business selling pictures of actresses, fighters, and the sporting gentry of the day.

The seamier side of life in Manhattan was a by-product of the city's slums which bred criminal types antagonistic to society and girls who would "go wrong" gladly to escape the dreary monotony of their everyday lives.

John Allen, known as the "Wickedest Man in New York," ran a dance house on Water Street where the neighborhood bullies found their pleasure in well-upholstered hoydens.

The uptown gambling palaces, where a fortune could be staked on the turn of a faro card, catered to the gentry who were supplied with the best in food and drink.

New York's public servants have always earned their keep. In the days following the Civil War, police worked in pairs through tough districts like the Tenderloin, the Bowery, or the lower East Side but they often needed reinforcements when enraged mobs tried to take back their own (*above*). Ambulances rolled day and night to tend the victims of traffic accidents (*upper right*). Firemen continually had their hands full (*right*). The worst fires of the period occurred in tenement houses, crammed with people, where open airshafts made perfect drafts for the leaping flames which turned the buildings into infernos.

116

The Biggest City in the Midwest, Chicago Was the Great

FUR COATS were the order of the day in Chicago when bitter winds from Lake Michigan swept the streets of the great metropolis sprawled along the water front. Second in size of America's cities, this key to the Midwest was possessed of a fierce, coarse energy which showed to best advantage in the rapid rebuilding program after the devastating fire of 1871.

Food and Grain Merchant to the United States Population

Chicago was over the million mark by 1890, a strong concentration of Germans and Scandinavians pushing up the figure. The city was the center of America's railroad network, feeding the east and west coasts with impartiality. Teeming cattle pens, vast lumber yards, and grain elevators filled to repletion gave the city its commercial character and businesslike air.

The Mellow and Distinctive Cities of Middle America All

THE GAUDY riverboat which symbolized pre-Civil War America and Mark Twain's country helped make many American cities famous. Among them were Pittsburgh (pages 106-107), at the confluence of the Allegheny and Monongahela Rivers, where the Ohio began; Cincinnati (*below*), on that river; St. Louis (*right*), edging the mighty Mississippi; and New Orleans (*lower right*), last stop on the big waterway.

The Civil War brought big changes. War itself disrupted commerce but its main significance lay in its dates, for these marked the start of the enormous railroad boom. As steel rails linked East, West, North, and South, the steamers were doomed.

Fortunately, most of the Midwestern cities did not die with the river craft. Some became railroad centers, adept at storing and handling freight. Others turned to manufacturing.

Situated near rich coal fields, Pittsburgh became a major industrial center for the manufacture of iron and steel, its smoking suburbs extending for miles up the riverbanks. Petroleum too, from nearby wells, bulked large in the economy of the city, reaching it in barrels carried by barge, before the growth of the pipe lines.

St. Louis, fifth city in America, grew into a major rail center. Cincinnati turned to slaughterhouses and breweries. Only New Orleans failed to regain its prewar glory. Cotton bales piled its wharves, but not in the rich profusion of the past.

120

Watched the Passing of the Riverboats with Great Sorrow

While Midwestern Cities Were Suffering Growing Pains, There Was a Surge of Activity in the Far West

PLEASANT cities dotted the Great Lakes area in the booming days following the Civil War, and they were slowly caught up in the tempo of the times. Detroit (*right*), Buffalo (*below*), Cleveland, and Toledo turned out steel, chemicals, pharmaceuticals, and manufactured goods, but their peak development did not come until after the turn of the century.

Easterners looked with interest at the two great towns beyond the Mississippi, Salt Lake City and San Francisco. The former stood as a personal monument to the magnetic Brigham Young, stern leader of the Mormon sect.

San Francisco reigned as queen of the Pacific. This was a dynamic metropolis, richly cosmopolitan, serving as a clearing house for precious metals from nearby mines and agricultural produce from the rich valleys.

Set between gleaming mountains and a giant lake, Salt Lake City (*below*) was turned into an earthly paradise by its hard-working founders. San Francisco, on rolling hills above the bay (*above*), looked past the Golden Gate to the Pacific and the Far East with its wonders.

RURAL AMERICA

To NEW ENGLAND intellectuals, poets who lived in cities, and artists, farm life was a picturesque idyll (*above*). In actual fact, rural living meant a never-ending round of strenuous work and long hours. The farmer rose before dawn to tend his livestock and accomplish the chores of daily living, then spent the day in the fields, often reaching the dinner table only after night had fallen.

In return for his labor, the farmer gained a precarious living. The sturdy independence so highly valued by the tiller of the soil was a deep-rooted American tradition.

From 1865 to 1900, acreage under cultivation shot up at a dizzy rate, and the latter year saw six million farms in the United States. Opening up of western lands in Kansas, Nebraska, North and South Dakota, and other states and territories accounted for much of the increase in agricultural production.

124

JUST before the Civil War, there were 31 million people in the United States and by 1900 the figure had spiraled to 76 million. American farmers raised enough food for the population increase throughout this period, and had produce left over for export. But the farmer's lot was far from happy.

At the root of the trouble were declining prices and a steady falling off of farm income. Cultivation of the great plains led to disastrous overproduction and the price structure crumbled further when the U.S. farmer sent his grain into competition with bumper crops from Australia, Canada, and Russia.

Rural workers got little for what they sold but paid heavily for what they bought. Safe from European competition because of high-tariff walls, eastern manufacturers kept the price of their goods up and farmers had to reach deep into their pockets when they needed pots and pans or agricultural machinery.

Caught as he was, the toiler of the plains went into debt. Hundreds of thousands of American farms were heavily mortgaged to the moneylenders of the East.

Among the farmers' bitterest enemies were the railways, which charged exorbitant rates when they could, and the middlemen who were constantly seeking to corner markets, to the disadvantage of the men who raised the crops.

Natural ills besetting the farmer included drought, dust storms, prairie fires, and overwhelming plagues of insects. When clouds of grasshoppers descended on the plains, they were raked into piles and burned (*below*) or shoveled into deep trenches and buried.

CATTLE and beef were prime products of the enormous plains area stretching from the Mississippi to the Rockies and from the Rio Grande to Canada.

Texas ruled supreme as cow country and produced a specialized breed of cowboys all its own (pages 276-283).

Two factors made the huge cattle industry possible and profitable: extension of the railways west, and mile upon open mile of grazing land in Kansas, Colorado, Montana, Wyoming, and neighboring territories. Just after the Civil War, the railroads pushed west into Kansas. Cattle ranchers in Texas could then drive their huge herds north, fatten them on acres of free land in the public domain and when they had reached marketable weight, run them into cattle cars for the journey to the packing houses in the Midwest.

Cattle drives, up such memorable paths as the Chisholm and Bozeman Trails, were earth-shaking events as thousands of beasts pounded the earth into dust in the great trek north. Terminal points for the drives were such scarlet towns as Wichita, Abilene, and Dodge City in which cowboys liquored up, dallied with fancy ladies, and bucked the dealer at seven-card stud.

Ranchers seeking bonus prices for cattle kept their longhorns in Kansas corrals for a period (*above*). They were fattened on corn and their meat was prime.

Corn, most of which went to feed cattle and hogs, had moved west as had wheat. Grain-producing states such as Pennsylvania, Ohio, and Wisconsin saw the flatlands of the Mississippi and Missouri River valleys displacing them as producers of the huge cereal crops.

Kept City Tables Well Supplied with Beef and Bread

Wheat farmers toiled under the bright blue sky of Dakota Territory (*above*) to produce grain which filled the great elevators of the Midwest and East (*below*). New agricultural machinery, much of it steam powered, helped ease their labor over the wide plains.

WHILE ten-thousand-acre farms and sweeping cattle ranches of the country beyond the Mississippi caught the public eye, everyday farming moved on in its prosaic way throughout the East and Midwest. Fruit farming proved profitable and October saw grapes being gathered from Hudson Valley vineyards (*above*), pumpkins and squash collected in Indiana, and the rich apple harvest of Michigan. Florida, in competition with California, turned to intensive cultivation of citrus fruit, and southern oranges and grapefruit began to appear on Victorian breakfast tables to give tropical touches to the solid morning fare.

Other breakfast foods, such as bacon and milk, came from middlemen who ringed the larger cities with processing plants. New Jersey's abattoirs (*right*) and New York state creameries (*upper right*) took raw produce from the farmer and turned it into salable food for city dwellers whose number was increasing at such a rate that America's population doubled in a single generation.

The middleman's profit, along with declining soil fertility, the high cost of bank loans, and continually depressed farm prices, did much to depopulate large rural areas in the East and, to a lesser extent, the Midwest.

Truck farmers and livestock breeders lingered on to supply the cities but the promise of new, virgin soil and cheap land caused many an eastern farmer to hang a "Gone to Kansas" sign on his front door and light out for faraway places. The lure of the city too helped depopulate eastern farms. New generations were quick to trade the uncertainties of rural life for the sure pay of urban factories and the many pleasures of city life.

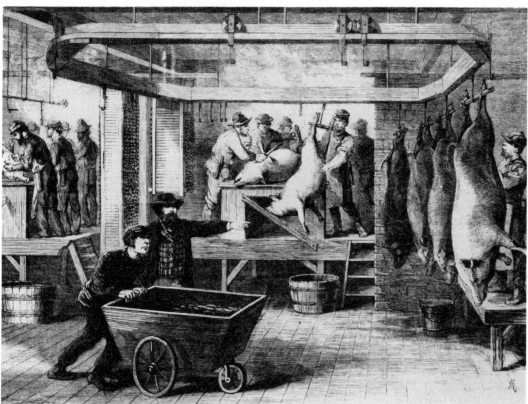

Hopeful Signs Abounded in the "New South" but the Climb Back to Relative Prosperity Was a Long One

THE SOUTH kept to its agricultural ways, for the most part, in the years after the Civil War. Breaking up of large plantations yielded cheap land for any who could afford it, and the number of farms reached 1½ million by 1880, twice the prewar figure. The number was somewhat misleading, for the poor white like the Georgia "cracker" shown below might till but three or four acres, and yet call his holdings a "farm." Still, the painful accumulation of hard-earned cash, perhaps from share-cropping, let many a southerner purchase land of his own for the first time.

Scratching the worked-out soil for subsistence, the small farmer had all he could do to put in a money crop to bring him a few needed dollars each year. Tobacco, hogs, or chickens sometimes served these ends.

On the larger farms, diversification of crops was practiced more and more. Southern food produce—Georgia peaches and melons, pecans from the Gulf Coast, citrus fruit from Florida—found its way north. The sugar-cane harvest in Louisiana (*right*) kept nearby refineries working. Lowland areas of South Carolina produced rice.

Cotton, despite the agronomists who preached diversification, remained king and farmers gathered in groups to examine the first bale of the season's crop as it came from the press (*lower right*). By 1871, 4,300,000 bales of the white fiber were produced annually by southern farms, a figure which showed a significant advance over prewar days. As long as prices remained high, as they did just after the war, the cotton boll would symbolize Dixie.

Rural Pleasures Were Simple Ones but They Broke Up
Much of the Monotony of Farm and Small-town Life

BUCOLIC joys were strenuous and hearty, made sweeter by the long intervals which separated them. The farmer's life was necessarily a lonely one. Small-town rural living meant an unvarying day-to-day routine.

Certain holidays created high spots in the monotonous year, among them the Fourth of July. Fried chicken and corn bread with homemade ice cream provided a solid base for floods of patriotic oratory and nerve-jangling fireworks.

Autumn was the most exciting season as harvest time brought rich opportunities for work and play. After a day in the fields harvesting pumpkins and shucking corn (*lower left*), crowds gathered for events like apple bees (*left*) at which the freshly-picked fruit was pared and dried for market.

At threshing time, farmers pitched in to help each other pick and process grain. Each farmhouse in turn was host to the crew, and it became a point of honor for each farm wife to provide the best she had to offer. Roasts of pork, bowls of chicken fricassee, slabs of bacon, with mounds of pancakes and dumplings swimming in syrup, disappeared quickly, and fiddles were brought out for entertainment. In this season also were state and county fairs, at which farm families might meet each other once a year.

In winter, small-town folk bundled themselves into straw-filled sleighs for trips over the white countryside (*below*), while farm boys hunted on the snow-filled fields and skated up the brooks and ponds.

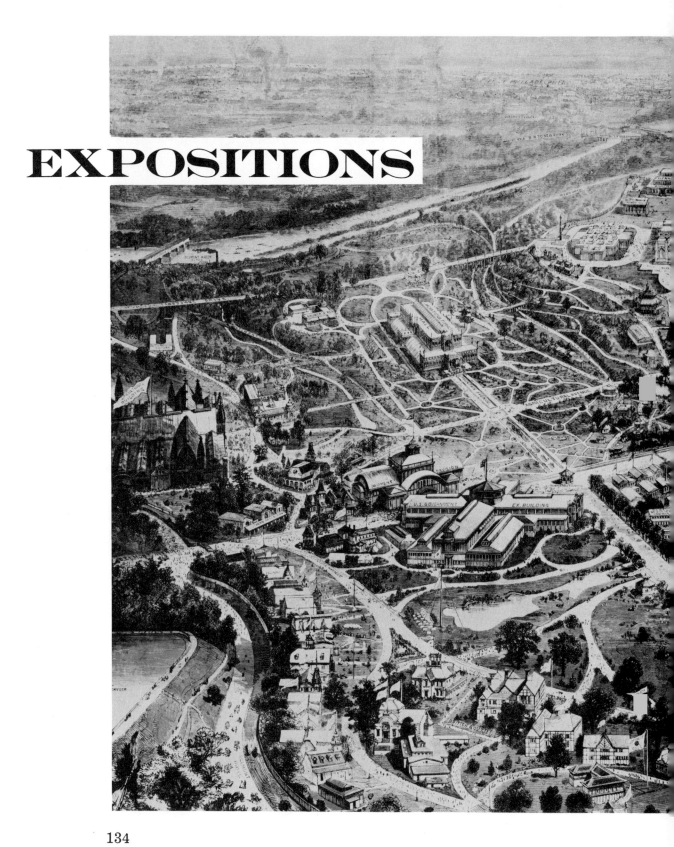

EXPOSITIONS

136

In 1876, Millions of Americans Flocked to Philadelphia to Marvel at the Wonders They Had Wrought in 100 Years

Dom Pedro appeared and mounted the platform, to be followed by President and Mrs. Grant, who were greeted by the "Grand Centennial March," composed for the occasion by Richard Wagner.

One thousand singers chanted John Greenleaf Whittier's "Centennial Hymn." The exhibition was presented to the President, who made a brief response. The American flag unfurled.

After a short tour of the important buildings, President and Emperor entered Machinery Hall and stood before the great Corliss engine, the colossus of the exhibition (*left*). As both men turned the valves, the great walking beams began to move and the International Exhibition of 1876 was open.

Multitudes came from all over the nation, taking advantage of cut-rate railroad fares to reach Philadelphia and gape at the marvels it presented. Irate citizens battled for hotel rooms in the usually placid Quaker City (*upper left*) and jostled each other as they ran for the horsecars each evening (*lower right*) which took them into the heart of downtown.

F AIRS and expositions are dear to the American heart. They got off to a flying start in 1876 as the nation celebrated its hundredth birthday with the Centennial Exposition at Philadelphia.

Three years in the planning, the undertaking was the largest thing of its kind ever to occur in the world, a source of great satisfaction to the nationalistic American mind.

Opening-day ceremonies matched the scale of the huge exposition in scope and impressiveness. President Grant presided, assisted by Dom Pedro, Emperor of Brazil and the first major foreign potentate ever to visit the United States.

More than a hundred thousand people passed through the gates and stood in a surging mass before Memorial Hall.

The Centennial Exhibition Was Rich in Handicrafts
But Was Woefully Lacking in Architectural Elegance

Typical of the exhibition was the architecture of the Agricultural Hall, which had cost $300,000. Covering over ten acres, the wood-and-glass building had a cathedral-like nave crossed by three transepts, each made up of Gothic truss arches. Under this unlikely construction, Victorian fountains splashed into ornamental pools to universal delight.

A STATISTICIAN's dream, the exposition produced an imposing array of figures, most of them huge by Victorian standards.

Covering 236 acres of Philadelphia's Fairmount Park, the exhibition cost 10 million dollars and lasted from May to November. Paid admissions totaled 8 million; free ones, almost 2 million. Some 190 buildings dotted the grounds (pages 134 and 135) and thirty-one foreign nations were represented. Spectators walked or rode over seven miles of paths and drives, and a narrow-gauge steam railway ran over five and one-half miles of track.

Seven major buildings offered exhibits on Mining and Metallurgy, Manufacturing, Education and Science, Art, Machinery, Agriculture and Horticulture, and there was an impressive Women's Pavilion in addition. The mammoth Corliss engine drew visitors like a magnet; it weighed eight hundred tons and its power drove eight thousand different machines.

Contemporary writers were carried away by the sights: "The colossal proportions of the main building struck every visitor's wondering attention—relieved, however, by its exquisitely artistic form and endless expanse of complementary colors—and, within, a universe of the wonderful and beautiful such as the eye of man never before beheld nor his hand created."

Such rhapsodies were ill deserved. The main buildings, huge as they were, loomed as graceless, awkward, ugly structures devoid of charm and weak in architectural form. Smaller artifacts, like the mineral-water fountain and the inkstand shown at right, showed the depths to which a nation's handicrafts could fall.

The European nations' exhibits made up for America's lack of cultural achievement. Queen Victoria sent a group of etchings from her own hand.

Dr. CARVER SHOOTING.

HURDLE RACING

NORTHERN PACIFIC R.R.

EXHIBIT FROM THE GREAT WHEAT COUNTRY

ELKS TROTTING IN HARNESS

ON THE ROAD TO THE FAIR.

SUCCESS at Philadelphia gave inhabitants of other cities and states ideas and a rash of fairs and exhibitions swept the United States. The Cincinnati Centennial featured a 1,500-foot-long Machinery Hall traversed by a stream holding Venetian gondolas. In the mid-eighties, New Orleans celebrated with a cotton exposition at which visitors exclaimed in wonder at the Japanese porcelain, lacquerware, and prints which brought a touch of the faraway East to America (*left*).

Rich in native traditions were the state fairs such as the Minnesota Fair at St. Paul pictured on the opposite page. Farmers hitched their teams to take entire families for all-day outings, rubbing shoulders with Indians and city visitors at these displays of rural plenty. Glossy-coated horses, hogs fattened to bursting, life-size cows carved from creamy butter, piles of gourds all attested the rich bounty of America.

141

In a Panic Year of the Gay and Wicked Nineties, Chicago Put on a Show Which Dazzled the Nation

CHICAGO, dedicated to doing things bigger and better than her sister cities, reached a pinnacle in 1893 as she played host at the opening of the World's Columbian Exposition, honoring the discovery of the New World. The opening ceremonies on May 1, led by President Cleveland, carried echoes of Philadelphia in 1876:

"As the President touched the button there arose from all sides a wild outburst of sound, the people and the orchestra uniting in the triumphant strains of Handel's 'Hallelujah Chorus,' while the wheels of the great Allis engine in the Machinery Hall began to revolve and the electric fountains in the lagoons to play. Torrents of water gushed from the great McMonnies fountain, the artillery thundered salutes and the chimes of the Factories Hall and German Building rang merry peals, while conspicuous in the Court of Honor the golden beauty of the 'Republic' stood discovered. At the same moment the flags in front of the platform parted, revealing the gilded models of the Columbian caravels."

There was one enormous advance over the Philadelphia Exposition; in Chicago, the architects did themselves proud, despite their lack of innovation.

Eminent practitioners such as John W. Root, D. H. Burnham, Richard M. Hunt, and Charles F. McKim used gleaming white plaster to create a city of related classical buildings set amid lagoons, basins, and ponds. Even pioneer Louis H. Sullivan was represented by his striking Transportation Building (page 194).

Awe-struck visitors, straw-hatted and nattily dressed in white (*right*), could journey over blue water in Venetian splendor (*upper left*) in the shadows of the snowy structures.

After dark, the Midway Plaisance glowed with wickedness under the dancing lights of the huge 250-foot Ferris wheel (*lower left*). Oriental dancing girls, Egyptian fakirs, Algerian and Persian merchants beckoned and enticed the 12 million who saw the fair.

SPEECHLESS.

143

DISASTER

145

THE DECADES following the Civil War were rife with catastrophe. *Frank Leslie's Illustrated Newspaper* carried a weekly column of accidents, presenting in text and pictures a list of ship collisions, train wrecks, fires, escapades of mad dogs and escaped bulls, murders, suicides, and street fights.

The saga of man against the sea loomed large in Victorian days as travel between the United States and Europe increased. Many a steamer and sailing ship grounded on treacherous ledges between Capes Cod and Hatteras, and the Atlantic Coast was patrolled by men of the more than 200 stations established by the United States Life-Saving Service.

Members of the seven-man station crews walked the sands, watching for distress signals which brought out the heavy surfboats for launching (*above*). If the water was too rough for small craft, lines were fired to the stranded vessels and passengers were brought safely ashore by the breeches buoy.

Farther out at sea, luck ruled the waves. When the Cunard liner *Oregon* was struck by a passing schooner off Fire Island on March 14, 1886, and began to sink, her signals were seen by the pilot boat *Phantom*, which stood by to rescue passengers. With the aid of the coasting schooner *Fannie E. Gorham*, and the North German Lloyd's liner *Fulda*, 896 crew members and passengers were saved before the great ship plunged to the bottom (pages 144-145).

Fire at sea was an ever-present threat. It caused terrible disasters on ferryboats and excursion steamers, loaded with women and children.

River water, too, held a menace, and inhabitants of middle America often saw the Missouri, Mississippi, and Ohio Rivers on wild rampages flooding lowland areas and bringing silt by the ton into the streets of Cincinnati, Louisville, St. Paul, and other major cities.

146

In the summer of 1880, the ferry *Seawanhaka*, carrying gentlemen to and from their New York City jobs, burst into flame a few yards from shore and thirty lives were lost. Mortality rates in the South climbed when the muddy Mississippi overran its banks (*below*), and ancient riverboats steamed to the rescue of those marooned in houses.

CHICAGOANS lived through a red nightmare on October 8-9, 1871, as a sweeping, out-of-control fire destroyed the city. Starting in a frame structure on the West Side, the blaze set off the lumber yards, then, carried by raging winds, ran through the South Side and leaped the river to blaze fiercely through the North Side in its thirty hours of progress.

Seen from the water, the conflagration was a fearful sight (*above*) as it ravaged hotels, railroad stations, theaters, stores, residences, municipal buildings, and elevators stored with millions of bushels of grain. "In many places the solid granite had cracked and peeled in great flakes, like stucco in the frost," said a spectator. "The iron castings are partly melted and partly twisted into forms of startling grotesqueness. I have seen fluted columns, bell wires, gas and water pipes, wreathed and twisted among the smoul-

148

Worst of the City Fires in Our United States History

dering ashes of a cellar like a coil of snakes of assorted sizes."

Families perished on rooftops (*right*), their screams unheard in the night. More fortunate people fled to Lincoln Park and the cold waters of Lake Michigan. The restless inferno burned the Crosby Opera House (*below*), the Gold Coast mansions, and the dives of Conley's Patch with equal impartiality.

When the flames ran out, a specter city greeted the dawn (*bottom*). More than 17,000 buildings were gone.

In the Late 1880s the Great Johnstown Flood Entered Our

Language as a Symbol of Devastation by Raging Waters

TERROR rode through western Pennsylvania on May 31, 1889, when a burst dam in the Conemaugh River Valley let loose a wall of water fifty feet high and a half mile wide on the city of Johnstown.

Historian E. B. Andrews reported the scene: "Trees, brush, furniture, boulders, pig and railway iron, corpses, machinery, miles and miles of barbed wire, and an indescribable mass of miscellaneous wreckage, all inextricably mixed, . . . freighted the torrent. Immense mills were knocked from their foundations, and whirled down-stream like children's block-work. Pig iron by the hundred tons was borne away, the bars subsequently strewn for miles down the valley. Engines weighing twenty tons were tossed up and on as if the law of gravity had been repealed. One locomotive was carried a mile. At Johnstown, where the shape of the valley generated an enormous whirlpool, the roar of the waters and the grinding together of the wreckage rent the air like lost spirits groaning in chorus."

Hard-driving rains, pelting for days, had swelled the reservoir, 250 feet above the city. The thirty thousand inhabitants had scant warning of the approaching waters and several thousands lost their lives.

News of the disaster spread around the world and relief poured into the stricken city from Europe and Pennsylvania's sister states. New York City and Philadelphia gave a half million dollars each. Total contributions reached three million.

Criminal elements in the city attempted looting on the heels of the flood but were turned back by troops (*upper left*). Debris littered the flats near the river (*below*) or piled up against the railway bridge and caught fire, burning for some twelve hours (*lower left*).

151

PASSENGERS on railroads during the years before the turn of the century took chances with the vagaries of nature. Forest fires in Maine (*above*), floods in the Mississippi Valley, blizzards in Michigan, dust storms and Indians on the Great Plains all made following the iron horse a perilous enterprise.

Man-made ills were worse. In one two-month period, just after the Civil War, a locomotive ran through the rear of a passenger car on the Housatonic River Railroad in Connecticut; two Long Island Railroad trains crashed head on; a Rensselaer and Saratoga Railroad train plunged into a river at Troy, New York; and an entire train left the track and rolled onto its side at Auburn, in the same state.

Disaster plagued the Hudson River Railroad in 1882, and the Boston and Providence in 1887. In September of that year, the Midwest saw a national tragedy on the Toledo, Peoria and Western near Piper City, Illinois, in which 160 people were killed when the train plunged through a burning wooden bridge.

Inadequate signaling systems, tracks with blind curves, and poor brakes brought on most crashes. A flood of new inventions made rail travel comparatively safe by the nineties.

152

Flaming Forests and Uncontrollable Floods Put
Major Obstacles in the Paths of Early Railroad Men

The Piper City disaster involved a train carrying 960 passengers from Peoria and central Illinois on an excursion to Niagara Falls. Nearing a flaming trestle bridge, the engineer tried in vain to stop the cars in time. Relatives were rushed to the scene of the tragedy.

Nature Loosed a Gigantic Fall of Snow over New York
In 1888, Creating a Blizzard to Be Talked of for Years

THE "Blizzard of '88" fell upon New York City on March 12, burying the metropolis under a winter blanket and paralyzing business and traffic. Policemen rubbed the ears of passers-by to prevent frostbite, and an occasional citizen died of overexertion or exposure.

Drifts piled up to fifteen feet and those who shoveled out the city throughout the week (*left*) lit bonfires in holes in the snow to help ease their task.

Schools, the Stock Exchange, the Subtreasury, and most businesses closed down by noon and on the following day, thousands crossed the ice-bound East River on foot. The great storm was an annoyance rather than a disaster.

154

Capital and Labor

INDUSTRY

Abundant High-quality Steel Laid the Foundations For United States Leadership in the Field of Industry

FLAME spewing from the mighty Bessemer converters at Pittsburgh (*left*) as molten iron was changed into steel was a fit symbol for the industrial might of nineteenth-century America. The huge vessels were largely replaced by open-hearth furnaces after the turn of the century, but Bessemer steel made the United States the biggest manufacturing country in the world.

Burly immigrants from eastern Europe stoked the Pennsylvania coke ovens (pages 156-157) and sweated under the lurid glare of the converters to make their new nation the number one steel producer. The prince of this inferno-like domain was a soft-spoken, Scotch-born capitalist, Andrew Carnegie (*upper right*).

Carnegie worked in a cotton mill as a boy; as a telegrapher; and for the Pennsylvania Railroad. He was of humble origin. Once he invested his carefully saved money in the steel business, his rise was swift and sure. By 1879, six years after Carnegie entered the business, U.S. steel production topped nine hundred thousand tons.

Iron ore from Michigan, Minnesota, and Wisconsin; Great Lakes steamers for transportation; and Pennsylvania's coal fields made America a natural steel producer. Gradually Carnegie acquired partial control of these elements and built the Carnegie Steel Company which, by the turn of the century, produced one-quarter of the steel turned out in the United States.

Able lieutenants such as Henry C. Frick, chairman of Carnegie's company, rode labor hard and created stiff anti-union policies. During the Homestead Strike of 1892, Frick narrowly escaped death (*right*) at the hands of assassin Alexander Berkman.

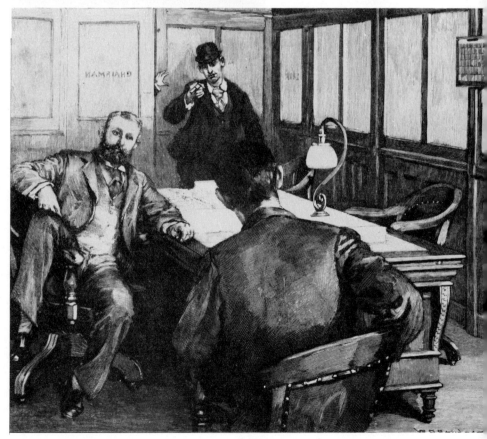

159

160

Hard-driving Capitalists Seeking Personal Empires
Created a Vast and Efficient Railway Network

CORNELIUS VANDERBILT (*above*), once a ferryboat captain plying from Manhattan to Staten Island, turned an interest in steamboats into 10 million dollars before and during the Civil War. When he died in 1877, he had 100 million dollars. Railroads made the difference.

Across the nation, the post-bellum days were ripe ones for railroad building. In the East, Vanderbilt bought up small lines, consolidated them into the New York Central and, by 1873, could offer a through route from New York to Chicago. Under J. Edgar Thomson, the Pennsylvania linked the two great cities, as did the Erie and the Baltimore and Ohio.

The key year in western railroading was 1869, when the Union Pacific, building west, and the Central Pacific, building east, linked up near Ogden, Utah, to join Nebraska and California. For the first time, the railroad spanned the continent.

Once begun in earnest, railroad construction mounted at a dizzy rate. South of the Canadian border, the Northern Pacific joined Minnesota and Washington, running across the top of the nation. It was paralleled by the Great Northern, creation of James J. Hill (*above*), one of the kings of western railroading.

In the Southwest, the Atchison, Topeka and Santa Fe followed the old Santa Fe trail, and the Southern Pacific connected New Orleans and San Francisco. By 1900, the snorting iron horse (*left*) could use more than 193,000 miles of track within the United States.

To encourage railroad construction, the Federal government was free with land grants, which some railroads turned to profit; and financial aid, in the form of loans.

161

162

Black Gold Trapped Beneath the Pennsylvania Earth
Built Fortunes and Helped Produce a Classic Trust

JOHN D. ROCKEFELLER (*center*) turned crude oil into dollars. He did it by astute manipulation of companies and people, hiring brains to work with and for him, coldly suppressing competition and custom-tailoring business organizations to fit his own needs.

Rockefeller's result was the logical culmination of an increasing tendency toward centralization prevalent in American business. It had begun when the faceless corporation replaced single ownership and old-fashioned partnerships. The corporation promised advantages: it had perpetual life and could issue stock in quantity, bringing in as much capital as was needed. Further, corporations were limited-liability concerns; in case of failure, individuals were liable only to the amount of their stock holdings, not for the entire capitalization of the company, as was the case with partnerships.

Next came the pool, in which several concerns joined to divide up business; this was favored by early railroads as a means of eliminating competition and retaining a high price level. Pools worked well for a period.

On the heels of the pool was the great nineteenth-century business form, the trust. Several corporations turned their stock over to a board of trustees. These men ran the combine, and the original stockholders shared in dividends.

With huge capital resources brought about by combination, trusts could cut prices until competitors were driven to the wall; then set prices as they pleased. The big combinations operated efficiently, reducing duplication of effort and reaping the benefits of central control. Because of the immense amount of business they could place, trusts asked for and got special treatment from railroads. And their sheer size gave them powerful control over labor.

In 1865, the Pennsylvania oil fields were booming and Rockefeller entered the business. By 1870, the million-dollar Standard Oil Company of Ohio, operating in Cleveland, was under way. The young businessman soon found that oil production (*left*) was only a phase of the industry and there was enormous money to be made in refining, transportation, and storage. In partnership with Henry M. Flagler and others, Rockefeller procured freight rebates from the New York Central and Erie Railroads and began to force his competitors out of business.

The Standard Oil Trust was organized in 1879, and revised in 1882. Made up of forty companies, the properties combined under a single management controlled approximately 90 per cent of the refining and pipe-line capacity of the nation.

163

The Last Two Decades of the Nineteenth Century
Witnessed a Booming Growth of the Trust Movement

HARD on the heels of Standard Oil came a series of trusts—in lead, linseed oil, sugar, whisky, tobacco, and rubber. By 1899, there were 185 manufacturing combinations in the United States capitalized at a little over 3 billion dollars as against a total capitalization of almost 9 billion dollars for all manufacturing industries. Trusts controlled one-third of U.S. manufacturing capacity.

Other combinations, not necessarily trusts, sprang into prominence in the last decades of the nineteenth century. This was the age of "kings."

Despite the increasing use of steel for construction, lumber remained vital to the nation and giant logs felled in Wisconsin (*left*) and Michigan were hauled to rivers to be floated down to the sawmills. Prominent among the timber kings was Frederick Weyerhaeuser.

The "beef barons" were several in number and included Gustavus F. Swift, Nelson Morris and Philip D. Armour (*upper right*). Because of these men, beef cattle on the hoof (*lower right*) became porterhouse steak on eastern tables.

Armour, once a farmer and wholesale grocer, made his fortune selling meat during the Civil War, then looked about for new worlds. When the Union Stockyards were opened in Chicago in 1865, Armour moved in and by 1867, Armour and Brothers was becoming one of the nation's leading meat packers, noted for their efficiency in utilizing what were formerly waste products.

Swift pioneered in the use of refrigerator cars, carrying dressed meat from the big midwestern packing houses to the teeming eastern seaboard. Chicago, Kansas City, and Milwaukee became the meat capitals of the country.

165

Over the Huge Industrial Combinations of the Day
Lay the Long Shadow of the "Morgan Interests"

J. P. Morgan looked every inch the part of the powerful capitalist, dignified, beetle-browed and imposing as he sat behind his massive desk. He kept his own counsel and said little or nothing for publication. Reporters were turned away from his door with empty hands. The financier appeared indifferent to public opinion, and was often called aloof and reticent. His drive for acquisition created one of the major art collections in the United States.

IN NINETEENTH-CENTURY America, money was the great power which made the enormous trusts possible. The greatest of the financiers was John Pierpont Morgan, who had his hands deep in the American pie.

Born in a financial family, he was educated abroad, served an apprenticeship, and in 1871, joined with a respected Philadelphia organization to form the New York concern of Drexel, Morgan and Company. By 1895, he headed J. P. Morgan and Company and his name was the symbol of financial power around the world.

Morgan's brief words and decisive actions strongly affected the quotations of the New York Stock Exchange (*below*). To its members, he was known as "Jupiter," and it was a fitting title for the newest of the gods.

The "Morgan interests" had their hands in railroads, banks, shipping, steel, coal, utilities, insurance, and the other gigantic enterprises of the time.

Morgan picked up wrecked businesses, refinanced them, and placed his men on their boards of directors. In 1869, he fought Jay Gould and won in a battle for the Albany and Susquehanna Railroad; in 1885 he came to the rescue of the ailing Baltimore and Ohio. Morgan money backed James J. Hill. By 1890, "Jupiter" Morgan had played a part in the affairs of every major railroad.

When government credit proved shaky in 1895, as gold was drained away, Morgan supplied the precious metal to shore up the nation's finances. Just after the turn of the century, he formed the billion-dollar United States Steel Corporation which controlled 70 per cent of the iron and steel business of the country.

Speaking of the great financier's influence, a contemporary reporter said, "This is the nineteenth century idea of power . . . to draw up and hurl upon the industrial battlefield of modern society heavy cohorts of gold."

THERE was no unifying background among the men who controlled big business. A common democracy at the quick-lunch counters near Wall Street (*right*) where top-hatted financiers ate hurriedly, and a love of power, united them all. Beyond this, similarity ceased.

Daniel Drew, William W. Corcoran, Cyrus W. Field, and William B. Astor (*above, left to right*) were as different as black and white but typical of their times.

Drew was an unprincipled and scheming rogue who passed through the cattle and steamboat business on his way to Wall Street. As a director of the Erie Railroad, with his colleagues Jim Fisk and Jay Gould, he practiced large-scale, crooked stock manipulation but was turned on and crushed by his two partners. Going down to defeat in the Panic of 1873, Drew was bankrupt before his death.

Corcoran stood at the other end of the scale, a quiet, gentle man who began in the dry goods business and later amassed a fortune in banking. He retired in 1854, and until his death in 1888, managed his properties and indulged in numerous philanthropies. The Corcoran Gallery of Art in Washington became his legacy to the people of the nation.

The heart and soul of an adventurer animated Cyrus Field. His touch in the paper business was golden and he made money sufficient to retire on by the age of thirty-three. Inactivity was unthinkable to him and he came out of retirement to promote the Atlantic cable, the New York elevated, the Wabash Railroad, and a newspaper.

Astor lived eighty-three quiet years, investing inherited money in such prime property that he was known as the "landlord of New York."

168

Common People and the Great and Growing Middle Class

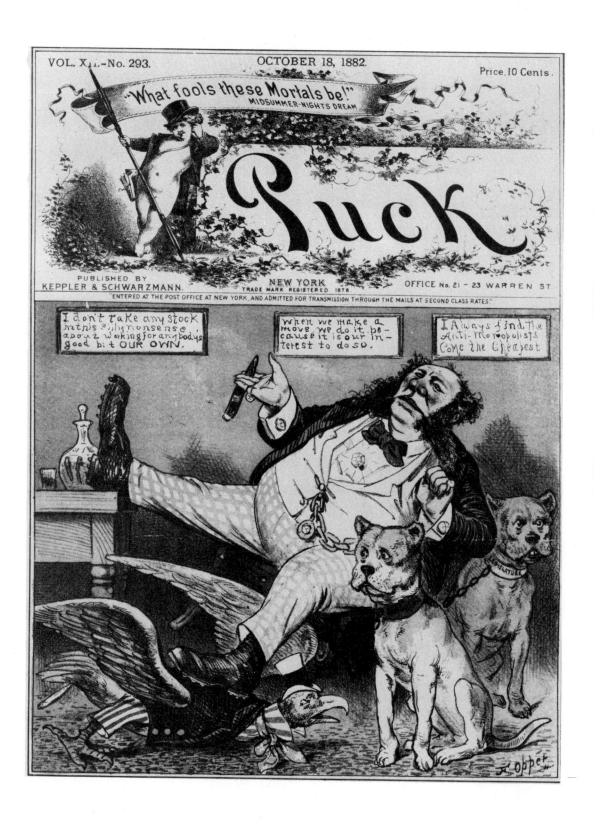

170

The Power of the Trusts and Their Indifference to the Public Interest Awakened America's Social Conscience

ON A DAY in 1882, William H. Vanderbilt, son of the Commodore, snapped out "The public be damned" to two reporters and was thoroughly lambasted by the press (*left*) as a result. The callous thrust of the statement jolted public opinion, which for years had been crystallizing against the behemoth of big business.

The capitalist became a bloated figure in newspaper cartoons, wearing a heavy gold watch chain and diamond stickpin and smoking a cigar. America was taken to task for worrying about the tiny scorpion of anarchy while the octopus of monopoly encircled the throne on which she sat (*below*).

The giant business combinations had created monopoly, but defended themselves, when they bothered to, by talking of more efficient operations and lowered prices. The question became: increased efficiency and lowered prices for whom? The savings from efficient operations were funneled back into the pockets of business. Lowered prices could be and were raised at the whim of the trusts, once they controlled the bulk of production.

As capitalism flowered and wealth became concentrated, the consumer realized his interests had been by-passed. The dilemma of labor was particularly difficult.

LABOR'S ROAD

174

Following the Civil War, Many Men Went West and Eastern Cities Turned to Europe for a Labor Supply

LABOR'S lot was a hard one. Big monopolies offered stringent terms on a take-it-or-leave-it basis and did not hesitate to blacklist men who agitated for fair treatment. Facing the power of the trusts was a labor supply with a heavy admixture of immigrants, unfamiliar with the language.

In 1864, Congress passed an act permitting U.S. contractors to import laborers from foreign countries, the laborers to turn over a portion of their wages until their passage across was fully paid. The American Immigrant Company was established in Connecticut and its representatives toured Great Britain, Germany, France, Belgium, and other nations, persuading low-paid European labor to try its lot across the water.

Newcomers to the land of plenty faced shocking living conditions. In Pittsburgh, their rickety frame dwelling places perched above the coke ovens (*left*). In the anthracite coal fields of Pennsylvania, immigrants began life anew in miserable hovels (*below*).

W. A Rogers.

176

Labor Conditions in the Garment Industry Were an Ugly Blot on the Nation in the Years Before 1900

MANY immigrants remained on the Atlantic seaboard to try their luck in the big cities. New York, by 1900, had a tenement population of one and a half million, the bulk of which was foreign-born. Huddled in their wretched homes, these new Americans provided an enormous labor pool which supplied the garment industry. Women and children carrying the piecework on which their lives depended (*left*) became common sights on Hester and Essex Streets.

Contractors for the major clothing manufacturers established the "sweating system," by which garments were cut and sewed in small shops or homes. If the "sweatshop" was established in a home, the entire family, plus boarders as well, shared the labor (*right*).

In 1893, a report to Congress on the system said that among homeworkers, "the women are more numerous than the men, and the children are as numerous as either. The work is carried out in the one, two or three rooms occupied by the family, which probably has, as subtenants or boarders, an equal number of outsiders. No pretense is made of separating the work from the household affairs, if such a term can be used to describe the existence of these people. The hours observed are simply those which endurance or necessity prescribe. Children are worked to death by the side of their parents, who are dying from overwork or disease."

In 1882, the Dress and Cloak Makers' Union was formed, largely of immigrants who made up the sweatshop population. The following year saw a strike in which garment workers called for $2.50 per day in wages and a working day of from 8 A.M. to 6 P.M. Piece-work was to be paid for at rates sufficient to enable each individual operator to earn $15 per week. Half of the strikers were women.

177

Early Attempts at Labor Organization Often Came to Nought, But One Strong Union Emerged from the Trials

Powderly (*left*) and Gompers (*right*) differed widely in their union philosophies but both agreed on the need for laws against child labor. Children were employed in the coal fields, often in freezing weather, to pick slate out of the crushed anthracite, as shown below.

UNIONIZATION was old in America in the 1860s, but there had been no successful major attempt to group unions together for mass economic and political action.

In 1866, the National Labor Union came into being under the hand of W. H. Sylvis. It was largely concerned with establishment of cooperative shops in which workers would supply their own capital and reap their own profits. The experiments met failure and the organization passed out of existence by 1872.

Made of stronger stuff was the Noble Order of the Knights of Labor, created at Philadelphia in 1869. The Knights began as a secret society, with grips and passwords, but soon passed through this early phase. The organization gained stature with the formation of a General Assembly in 1878 and election of Terence V. Powderly as Grand Master Workman in 1879. The new leader, looking more like an English vicar than an agitator, was a powerful firebrand and bore the stamp of "radical."

The Knights had the "one big union" concept, seeking to bring together skilled and unskilled labor alike and attempting to bring up the wages of the lowest-paid laborers. They advocated public ownership of utilities and establishment of producing cooperatives to make the nation's goods.

A successful railroad strike in 1885 helped swell membership, which reached 700,000 in 1886, but snubs from highly skilled workingmen, and the radical political program, led to the union's decline in the nineties.

Born in 1881, named in 1886, the American Federation of Labor became the solid union organization of the 1900s under Samuel Gompers. Made up of trade unions representing skilled workers, the Federation plumped for collective bargaining, the eight-hour day, better pay, and stiff labor laws. Its ends were economic rather than political and it permitted member unions to keep their autonomy. By 1900, the growing membership was over the half-million mark.

Disasters in the coal fields brought terror to laborers' families, and the United Mine Workers agitated for safe work conditions.

President Hayes Dispatched Troops to Pennsylvania, Maryland and West Virginia During the 1877 Strikes

AMERICAN workers turned to violence on a mass scale for the first time in the summer of 1877, creating the greatest strike in the nation's history. The disturbance ran through the United States like a jolting current.

The "great railroad strike" began in Martinsburg, West Virginia, when employees of the Baltimore and Ohio were asked to take a 10 per cent wage cut and work a reduced-hours schedule. Management called for the reduction, the second within a brief period, because of financial woes stemming from the Panic of 1873.

Trouble erupted at Martinsburg where railway workers attacked scab firemen and engineers (below), and quickly reached nearby Baltimore. News of the uprising sped over the telegraph and similar outbursts hit the Pennsylvania Railroad at Pittsburgh. In a matter of

days, the Erie and Lake Shore systems were affected and the trouble spread to Chicago, Buffalo, St. Louis, and San Francisco. General dissatisfaction with wages and hours ran like a prairie fire among railway men across the country.

Governors in the affected states panicked and called out local militia. Pittsburgh became the center of violence as Philadelphia troops entered the area. Rifles blazed into the mob at the Union Depot (pages 172-173) and blood dripped into the ties. That night, enraged strikers sent flaming oil and coal cars against a roundhouse and a depot (right), turning them into infernos.

Backed by bayonets, the railroads finally won out. Defeated workers accepted pay cuts and sent their trains highballing across the country. The strike cost over a hundred lives and 10 million dollars in property damage.

FRANK LESLIE'S

ILLUSTRATED

RAILROAD RIOT EXTRA.

NEWSPAPER

Entered according to the Act of Congress, in the year 1877, by Frank Leslie, in the office of the Librarian of Congress at Washington.

[Extra Number.] NEW YORK, AUGUST 4, 1877. [Price, 10 Cents. $4.00 a Year. 12 Weeks, $1.00.

PENNSYLVANIA.—THE STRIKE ON THE PENNSYLVANIA RAILROAD—A MOB BURNING TRAINS OF CARS AND RAILROAD PROPERTY AT THE ROUND HOUSE, NEAR PITTSBURGH, ON THE NIGHT OF SATURDAY, JULY 21st.—From a Sketch by John Donaghy.

During the Mid-eighties, American Labor Was on the

"THE GREAT UPHEAVAL" was the name given to the erupting violence which swept the labor scene in 1885 and 1886, a period of intense labor activity.

A brief period of prosperity ended with the business recession of 1884, and newly active unions moved to prevent wage cuts and keep men on the job. The following year saw the national unemployment figure at 2 million and union leaders seething for action.

The Knights of Labor struck Jay Gould's Wabash railway system three times during this period. They succeeded in the first two, and gained restoration of a wage cut and union recognition. The third strike became a bitter one, spreading through five states and subjecting striking railway men to rifle fire at East St. Louis (*below*). The Knights were decisively defeated.

There were 645 strikes in 1885, and over 1,400 the following year when

Move as Never Before, Making Its Mighty Power Known

610,000 workers were out. In 1886, the Federation of Organized Trades and Labor Unions (which was shortly to become the American Federation of Labor) called for a series of May Day strikes in support of the eight-hour day and were joined in this endeavor by the Knights of Labor. The common front presented by the two major union organizations affected more than three hundred thousand men.

"New York's finest" used night sticks in 1886, during a street transit strike, to open the way for scab-operated horse-cars (*below*). Manhattan was further enlivened by a mayoralty race that year in which labor played a part. Economist Henry George, who advocated a single tax on land to meet all costs of government, ran as a labor candidate on a reform ticket. He lost to Abram S. Hewitt, but his heavy labor vote enabled him to end up ahead of Republican Theodore Roosevelt.

The Haymarket Bombing in 1886 Marked a Black Day
On Which Organized Labor Suffered a Serious Setback

Chicago's workingmen, called to meet in protest over police action at the McCormick works, were urged to carry arms (*upper right*), and their guns blazed out as police charged after the bomb exploded. Many of the city's laborers were of Bohemian or German origin. Exiles from the latter country, many of them anarchists, lurked about the fringes of the unions.

THE MAY DAY demonstrations of 1886 were large in scale at Chicago and continued for several days. Unionists, joined together at the McCormick Reaper Works in demonstrating for the eight-hour day and union recognition, attacked scab laborers on May 3 as they left the plant. Police fired into the crowd, killing one man and wounding several.

An angry protest meeting was called for the evening of May 4, in Haymarket Square, to protest police brutality. Some three thousand people appeared. Violent speeches, calling for blood and vengeance, aroused the mob, which was ordered by the police to disperse. During the resulting confusion, a dynamite bomb exploded, killing one policeman; several others were fatally injured by the explosion or in the rioting which followed.

Eight anarchists were arrested. None was convicted of direct connection with the bomb-throwing but all were charged with fomenting violence. Four of the men met death by hanging, one committed suicide. Three were imprisoned, to be pardoned in 1893.

The affair prodded public indignation, which arose to fever pitch. Labor unions became confused with groups of foreign-born immigrants advocating overthrow of the government. Years passed before union men erased the stigma. The Haymarket affair may have stimulated dissolution of the Knights of Labor, who had political ends in mind.

There existed, in Chicago, a branch of an anarchist organization called the Black International, but its numbers were small, and there was no great infiltration of the major unions.

When Carnegie Steel reduced wages at Homestead, only a minority of workers were involved but the union came to their defense and armed violence broke out. Pinkerton detectives, hired to protect scab labor, traveled up the Monongahela in armed barges to attack the strikers but were overcome and forced to surrender, as shown above.

And the Courts Soon Intervened in the Pullman Strike

THE CARNEGIE Steel Corporation battled its workers at Homestead, Pennsylvania, in 1892 (*opposite page*), but the disturbance was forgotten by 1894 when the great Pullman strike made headlines.

The Pullman Palace Car Company, near Chicago, called for a wage cut. It was opposed by 4,000 Pullman workers of the American Railway Union under Eugene V. Debs (*left*). Rail workers were forbidden to handle trains carrying Pullman cars.

Rioting began in June. Aroused, President Cleveland obtained an injunction forbidding interference with trains carrying the mails. The U.S. Cavalry came in to escort trains from Chicago stations (*below*). Debs was arrested and eventually imprisoned for contempt of court.

As the nineteenth century drew to a close, some 1,200 strikes were disrupting American industry each year. Losses to capital and labor together, in the last two decades, reached the appalling figure of 450 million dollars. Like it or not, the nation saw that labor was to be reckoned with as a powerful and organized force.

The press, in general, didn't like it. American periodicals took a peculiar position, attacking monopoly and its evils and defending the workingman from exploitation, but holding back support from organized labor in action.

The *New York Times* lamented the evils of the garment makers' existence; *Harper's Weekly* lashed out at the abun-

dance of child labor in Pennsylvania's bleak mining country. But when labor moved, by direct action, to better its lot, it found itself lacking in journalistic support.

Cartoons, such as *Puck*'s picture above, labeled "It works both ways," pointed up a favored belief: organized labor would eventually kill the goose which laid the golden eggs.

Labor agitators were shown dressed as capitalists (presumably with money wrested from the workingman) and had full beards, staring eyes, faces indicative of foreign origin, and insolent manners to the employers they opposed. Not until after 1900 did labor garner strong press support.

The Arts in America

ARCHITECTURE

DOMINATING the architectural enterprises of the late 1800s was the construction of the Brooklyn Bridge (*left*), a job begun in 1869 and completed in 1883. The huge structure, whose 1,600-foot span arches over the busy East River, emerged with a stark beauty all its own because of its creators' attention to function and their refusal to add superfluous ornament. Hung from massive, simple granite piers, the powerful steel cables holding up the roadway achieve a light and airy grace which minimizes their obvious weight.

The bridge is a monument to family enterprise. Begun by John A. Roebling, an expert on steel cables, it was finished by his son Washington. The latter, after the "bends," or caisson disease, crippled him, took to his bed but directed the construction effort to completion. New York celebrated the bridge's opening with a magnificent water carnival.

The Brooklyn Bridge is an achievement in itself. It is all the more remarkable because its clean beauty, with the obvious touches of the engineer, appeared when America had reached the lowest point in its architectural history.

The nation wallowed in ugliness of the kind personified by the "wedding cake" structure shown below, which marked the entrance to a Brooklyn cemetery. To the gentry of the period, this was a fine and tasteful thing.

Such monstrosities exemplified the Victorian Gothic, a favorite style in which pointed roofs, truncated towers, hollow buttresses, and fancy arches were scattered without rhyme or reason throughout stone and wooden buildings. Ornament dominated design, covering simple lines with products of the jigsaw and foundries specializing in decorative ironwork.

The prevailing colors were drab and muddy. Chocolate browns, slate grays, and black predominated.

A Strong Eclecticism Dominated Nineteenth-century Architecture Until Henry H. Richardson Appeared

PUBLIC buildings, in the years after the Civil War, were often designed in the Eclectic Style, which was merely an excuse for indiscriminate borrowing from the past. Details taken from ancient and Renaissance buildings were mixed with weird effect.

Typical is the Army, State and Navy Building at Washington (*above*), done in the 1880s. The enormous granite pile, rich with clustered classic columns high above street level, was in a style defined as "Roman Doric, with original treatment." Inside were iron columns and pilasters, bronze balustrades, marble walls, Egyptian ornament and a slab taken from a temple at Pompeii.

It was the taste of the times which brought such ponderous structures into being. Newly rich titans of business and government called for housing similar to that which sheltered the Medici. Architects paid much attention to the pretentious façades, and let interiors follow the external form, to the detriment of lighting, space, and comfort.

A needed breath of air came with Henry H. Richardson, a southern-born architect who placed his original stamp on buildings of the Victorian era. He studied at Harvard and the Ecole des Beaux-Arts in Paris, began practice in New York in 1866, and later moved to Brookline, Massachusetts.

Richardson was a romantic, a sensuous man in love with life and color. Deeply attached to the solid architecture of the Romanesque, he adapted it to his own purposes and created a new kind of American building.

Contemporary builders, in copying the Gothic, were content with surface imitation. In adapting the Romanesque, Richardson started from the ground and built organically, as did the medieval builders. The purpose of the structure, and the plan of the interior, defined the building's ultimate form. Richardson's work was often heavy, for he loved the power and thrust of great stones, but it had honesty, utility, and a rugged simplicity of mass unusual in the Gilded Age.

Among Richardson's outstanding monuments were Trinity Church, Boston; Chicago's Marshall Field Wholesale Building; Sever and Austin Halls at Harvard; a Pittsburgh courthouse and jail; and part of the state capitol at Albany.

Smaller works of great simplicity, color, and charm included country homes of wood, railway stations, and a series of small libraries. The Crane Library, at Quincy, Massachusetts (*below*), shows the Richardson mark.

Solidly constructed, the building hugs the ground and pleases by its unpretentious appearance. Windows, no longer merely ornamental, are placed for functional reasons. Interior utility calls for an off-center entrance. The tower holds a spiral stair to the storage attic, illuminated by its own bank of windows. Such touches as rounded arches and courses of rough stone (*right*) were Richardson trade-marks.

Details from the Ames Building: Bedford & Kingston Sts Boston
H·H·Richardson·Archt.

Carved·Capitals·in·Entrance

Entrance on Bedford St.

Third·Story·Windows·

To Stir the Nation's Builders, an Architectural Genius

Appeared in the Midwest

RICHARDSON died at 48, in 1886, too soon to incorporate the new ideas in the air concerning steel construction for buildings. He left behind a host of imitators. The dashing Louis Sullivan was not an imitator, but he was inspired by the Brookline architect.

Born in Boston, educated at M.I.T. and the Paris Beaux-Arts, a one-time resident of France, Sullivan came to Chicago to trumpet the doctrine of "form follows function." Much of the young architect's work was carried out while he was a partner in the firm of Adler and Sullivan.

Low-cost iron and steel paved the way for new building forms in the late 1800s. The old stone buildings were limited in height by their weight and bulk. Upper walls and floors were all supported by the walls of the foundation; the higher the building, the thicker the foundation walls had to be. In buildings of any height, the supporting walls became so thick as to severely limit interior space on the lower floors. Steel construction, in which the framework carried the weight and the walls were mere curtains, changed the picture and made the skyscraper possible. Steel cables supported the necessary elevators.

Sullivan seized on steel frames for his tall Wainwright Building in St. Louis and the Prudential Building in Buffalo. His exterior forms were refreshingly free of Gothic or Renaissance ornament, as in the Chicago Auditorium (left), and truly followed the building's functional needs. New skyscrapers of the nineties, still partially plagued with decorative touches (right), owed much to Sullivan's pioneering.

Louis Sullivan's audacity created the Transportation Building (upper left) at the Columbian Exposition—a strikingly original structure.

195

France's Great Tribute to America Came in the Form of a Gigantic Piece of Architectural Sculpture

IN EVERY nation, the massive statue called "Liberty Enlightening the World" means America. It was a gift from the people of France and came about as the result of an idea from Edouard de Laboulaye, who sought a new world monument to commemorate both the French and American Revolutions. A popular subscription in France brought $200,000 to pay for the statue, and $300,000 was raised in America to finance the base and pedestal.

Alsatian Frédéric Bartholdi created the colossus (*left*), which is 151 feet high and weighs 440,000 pounds, the tip of the torch being 305 feet above the water. The statue's creator attended the official dedication of his masterpiece on October 28, 1886. Pouring rain dampened the spirits of President Cleveland and the onlookers, and the great fireworks display honoring the statue was put off until the first clear night (*below*).

197

PAINTING

THREE immensely talented American painters—Homer, Eakins, and Ryder—emerged in the late Victorian period but they were ahead of the taste of their times.

Sticky, story-telling genre pictures spelled art to the average man. Wealthy patrons of the arts turned to the agile brush of Sargent for portraits. When size and splendor were important factors, buyers thought of Asher B. Durand's castle-filled landscapes of imaginary places, or the vast, romanticized western scenes of Albert Bierstadt.

Despite a somewhat unfavorable climate, painters went their own way and a respectable amount of good work was produced in the seventies, eighties, and nineties. George Inness outgrew the Hudson River School, as did Homer D. Martin, and both men created rich landscapes reflecting the bounty of the American countryside. Muralists John La Farge and Elihu Vedder covered the walls of public buildings with imposing tableaus.

Impressionism had its American devotees in Childe Hassam, John H. Twachtman, and J. Alden Weir, but none of them reached the heights achieved by the French masters. In France, Mary Cassatt's sun-filled canvases were warmly appreciated. Expatriate James McNeill Whistler, who called London his home, aroused popular indignation with his delicate mood pieces.

198

Men and women studied together at New York's Art Students League, which was founded in 1875 by a group of students

dissatisfied with the policies of the National Academy of Design. The League, a nonprofit, self-governing society, gave courses in drawing, painting, and sculpture, and let fresh air into the studios so long dominated by strict academic rules stifling young painters.

200

WINSLOW HOMER has never been surpassed as a painter of outdoor life in America. Fascinated by the sea, he painted it in sunshine and storm, setting down smashing breakers, a fog-shrouded coast, and the eternal battle between man and nature.

A thoroughgoing naturalist, Homer reached his peak in a series of magnificent water colors, broadly handled and crisp in execution. Ranging the north woods, New York's rivers and back country, and the sun-splashed Bahamas, he froze moments in time on his paper: a leaping trout, a drinking deer, the trembling of great leaves in "Palm Tree, Nassau" (*left*).

Boston-born, Homer lived in New York and visited the American tropics but spent much of his time in his seaside studio at Prout's Neck, Maine. He covered the Civil War for *Harper's Weekly*.

Lacking Homer's charm in paint, but excelling him in artistic ability was the American realist, Thomas Eakins of Philadelphia. Cool, analytical, thorough, he respected form and defined structure solidly in his beautifully executed oils. There was none of the exotic in Eakins, who chose his subjects from the world about him: baseball, rowing, the prize ring, a chess match, the concert hall, a teacher at work as in "The Agnew Clinic" (*above*).

Eakins brought his work to fruition in oils, after careful pencil and water color studies. The umbers, siennas, and golden yellows of his low-keyed palette suggest Rembrandt, as does his careful approach, but he lacks the spiritual depth of the Dutch master. A series of penetrating portraits capped Eakins' work and they remain as monuments, oblivious to changing manners and tastes. He never flattered a sitter.

FAR FROM the mainstream of American realism was John Singer Sargent, who was born in Florence and spent much of his life in Paris and London.

Sargent lives in his portraits, which chronicle the rich and glittering society of the Victorian and Edwardian ages. He has been called only a surface painter, but his surfaces were beautiful ones, lovingly worked.

The influence of Monet and the impressionists is strong in the sparkling and luminous water colors of Spain, Italy, Bavaria, and America which came from Sargent's brush. Dappled and broken color, quickly laid on, reflected the painter's interest in the play of light on surfaces. If Sargent was not profound, he excelled in verve and charm, and left rich memoirs of his time. In "Madame X" (*left*), which shocked the taste of the day, Sargent summed up his achievement.

The antithesis of popular painting lay in the work of the enigmatic artist named Albert Pinkham Ryder. An American mystic, he probed deep beneath the surface of reality and left painting valued for its spiritual content rather than representational value.

Ryder's lonesome poetry was reflected in his subject matter: "The Forest of Arden," "The Lorelei," "The Temple of the Mind," "Pegasus." One of America's few religious painters, he created "Christ Appearing to Mary," "Resurrection," and "Flight Into Egypt" (*right*). The sea haunted him but it was a different ocean from that seen by Winslow Homer.

Layer after layer of paint built up Ryder's richly glowing surfaces which resemble enamel. Simple masses and somber colors, with a feeling akin to that of the primitives, help create the mysterious aura which surrounds Ryder's work.

203

WRITERS

RIP-ROARING journalism became part of the Victorian scene with the advent of Joseph Pulitzer (*above*).

Major papers were often carry-overs from before the Civil War but the editors were disappearing. James Gordon Bennett of the New York *Herald* died in 1872, as did Horace Greeley of the New York *Tribune*. In Manhattan, Whitelaw Reid carried on at the latter publication, while Charles A. Dana's *Sun* reached a high professional level. Other New York papers sharpened their reporting after the Civil War, and new publications of merit grew in Chicago, Philadelphia, and San Francisco.

Joseph Pulitzer, born in Hungary, reached success with the St. Louis *Post-Dispatch,* then in 1883 bought the New York *World* from Jay Gould and sailed into his competition. By 1890, the Pulitzer Building (*left*) was a measure of his success.

Behind Pulitzer's pedantic appearance lay a nice appreciation of the public taste and a flair for sensationalism. Human interest stories, crime report-

ing, and a headlong plunge into politics captivated readers; by 1895, William Randolph Hearst had purchased the New York *Morning Journal* to further the same type of popular appeal. When the two giants contended, "yellow journalism" was born and circulation figures soared.

Magazines flourished. *Harper's Weekly* featured the cartoons of Thomas Nast (*self-caricatured below*) whose vitriolic pen helped oust the Tweed Ring. *Scribner's Monthly,* which became the *Century* in 1881, joined with the *Atlantic* to publish new American authors. In 1883, Cyrus H. K. Curtis attracted housewives with his new *Ladies' Home Journal,* which reached immense popularity within a decade. *McClure's* began in 1893, starting a low-price-magazine vogue.

205

AMERICA'S magnificent writers of the golden age reached their afternoon following the Civil War. Many of them published, but the mighty works lay behind them. Every man on these two pages died in the eighties or nineties.

A strange hiatus in publishing struck the country after 1865. People yearned to believe in the world of dignity and decorum as set forth in the essays of Ralph Waldo Emerson (*above*), but the shock of the recent conflict, and day-to-day money grubbing, relegated graceful style and polished prose to students alone. Emerson traveled and lectured in the seventies, but a mental decline set in and he died in 1882.

Henry Wadsworth Longfellow (*upper right*) stood as another victim of the war. His mellow, golden meters fell on deaf ears, conquered by a rising flood of realism. The noble poet turned to translation, producing his version of

Dante's *Inferno* in 1867. He died in the same year as Emerson.

Of tougher stuff was James Russell Lowell, poet, essayist, and satirist, who had created the *Biglow Papers* and a procession of sharply critical essays. In postwar years he taught at Harvard, helped to edit the *North American Review,* and served as minister to Madrid and London before his death in 1891.

Dr. Oliver Wendell Holmes maintained his reputation for wit and vigor until death overtook him in 1894. He published *The Poet at the Breakfast Table* in 1872, and followed it with biographies and novels.

Walt Whitman continued his "barbaric yawp" with new editions of *Leaves of Grass* and other writing until paralysis in 1873 and death in 1892. Herman Melville of New York created *Billy Budd, Foretopman* in his late years but died in 1891, unheralded and relatively unsung.

Lowell (*upper left*) spent his ripe maturity spreading American prestige abroad; Holmes (*upper right*) remained in great demand as a speaker. Illness brought down Whitman (*lower left*); Melville (*lower right*) became a New York customs house inspector.

America's New Authors Turned to Psychology, Realism,

THE "NEW WRITING" followed widely divergent paths. Emily Dickinson, a lady in retirement, sent forth poems fragile in content and strong in emotion to sway later generations. Mark Twain, (*upper left*) created a rough, vigorous, witty prose to describe the swirling Mississippi, the warmth of small-town life, and the vagaries of Europe. Henry James (*above*) found the climate of England salutary, settling there to turn out his polished, penetrating novels of contrasting social orders. Historian Francis Parkman (*left*) set down the shining story of New France, describing the explorations of Canada's early settlers.

A strong trend toward regional writing became evident. Bret Harte (*right*) took the West as his domain and wrote of California's mining towns. George W. Cable described Louisiana's dark bayous and Creole life. In Joel Chandler Harris' *Uncle Remus* stories, American folklore achieved literary status.

Local Color, and Humor in the Century's Later Years

In *Progress and Poverty*, social reformer Henry George (*above, left*) achieved a miracle: a book on economics which had wide popular acceptance. William Dean Howells (*above, right*), brilliant editor of the *Atlantic*, promoted the cause of the realistic novel, producing *The Rise of Silas Lapham* as his own contribution to this new and influential school.

THEATER

THE THEATER ranked high as an entertainment medium in an era which lacked motion pictures, radio, and television. Few native playwrights of any stature appeared, but America was blessed with an abundance of fine actors in the late nineteenth century.

Shakespeare brought out the people of culture. By the end of the era, such audiences could watch the works of George Bernard Shaw and Henrik Ibsen.

Minstrel shows, begun before the Civil War, remained in constant demand. Vaudeville, featuring trained seals, dog and pony acts, and overacted dramatic bits, was helped on its way by Tony Pastor and B. F. Keith. In 1866, *The Black Crook*, a huge extravaganza, ushered in the American musical and New York's Niblo's Gardens became the headquarters for such entertainment.

Manhattan held the lead as a theater city, but every major town had a stock company. These died gradually in the face of "the road," as major actors began their barnstorming tours across the country.

Many an actor going on the road went out in a vehicle by Irish-born Dion Boucicault, the theater's man of all work. Actor and playwright, he wrote or adapted over three hundred pieces for the stage. Bronson Howard ranked high for his realistic native dramas like *Shenandoah*.

The period belonged to the actors rather than writers, and imports from abroad drew acclaim. Sir Henry Irving (*opposite page, costumed for* Becket) was the top when he toured with the gracious Ellen Terry (*left*). Ada Rehan, born in England, became an American leading lady known for her role as Rosalind (*below*) in *As You Like It*.

American Actors and Actresses Showed a High Level
Of Performance and Were Extremely Popular Abroad

IRVING and Terry made successful American tours, as did France's Sarah Bernhardt and Poland's Helena Modjeska. But the United States was enthusiastic about its own talent as well as the great practitioners from overseas.

Among the early successes were those celebrated by Charlotte Cushman, who left opera to appear on the stage when her voice weakened. She starred as Lady Macbeth, and often appeared in such men's roles as Romeo, Hamlet, and Cardinal Wolsey. Her contemporary, Edward L. Davenport, was known for his versatility, playing in everything from comedy to *King Lear*.

America's greatest actor in the Victorian period was Edwin Booth (*above,*

right). Known for his low-key rendition of Hamlet, he reportedly spurned the sweeping gestures and ranting delivery which characterized the great tragedians of the day. Booth achieved fame as Richelieu, King Lear, and Shylock as well as Hamlet.

In 1864, the actor leased the Winter Garden theater in New York for a series of Shakespeare productions, but he was forced to leave the stage temporarily after his brother, John Wilkes Booth, assassinated Abraham Lincoln. Edwin Booth returned in 1866; in 1869 he built the Booth Theater. A series of successful appearances in America and London climaxed his fruitful career and he died in 1893. Booth founded the

Player's Club, bequeathing it his New York home.

Lawrence Barrett (*opposite page, left*) was a fine American actor of great intensity. He often toured with Edwin Booth, playing Othello to Booth's Iago, and Cassius to Booth's Brutus.

Richard Mansfield, born of British parents, achieved fame as Richard III (*below*), as well as Dr. Jekyll and Mr. Hyde. In 1890, he starred in *Beau Brummel* and in 1898, in *Cyrano de*

Bergerac. Mansfield brought Shaw to the United States in the nineties.

Joseph Jefferson (*above as Bob Acres in* The Rivals) was the third of his name and obviously born to act. With the aid of Boucicault he made a starring vehicle for himself out of *Rip Van Winkle*.

213

The Comedies of Manners Always Proved Popular but Such New Radicals as Ibsen Found Audience Acceptance

The School for Scandal played Wallack's new theater at Broadway and Thirtieth Street, New York, in 1882. Lester Wallack, an actor and theater manager, played Charles Surface in the Sheridan work. James W. Wallack, the actor-manager's father, had a similar career and starred at Drury Lane before coming to America to manage rising acting companies.

THE POLISHED John Drew, scion of a theatrical family, was an urbane, witty player who starred in a series of comedies opposite Maude Adams (*above*). Miss Adams, fragile and lovely, began as an ingenue at sixteen and after her comedy appearances, reached stardom in Sir James Barrie's *The Little Minister* in 1897. She played in *L'Aiglon* in 1900 and achieved lasting fame after the turn of the century as *Peter Pan*.

Another glamorous lady of the American Victorian theater was the beautiful Mary Anderson (*left*). A fiery performer, Miss Anderson played Juliet, Lady Macbeth, and Rosalind, and starred in W. S. Gilbert's *Pygmalion and Galatea*. She retired while young, to marry.

215

Brazen Trombones and Thundering Drums Marked
The Glorious Appearance of P. T. Barnum's Attractions

BIGGER elephants, whiter whales, and the most luxuriantly bearded ladies had a way of ending up with Phineas Taylor Barnum, the genius of promotion in the show business world.

Barnum, who had been a bartender and had run a newspaper, started his show business career by exploiting an ancient colored woman who claimed to have been George Washington's nurse. He moved on to control the American Museum in New York City, then maintained a series of educational, sensational, and highly moral exhibits in his permanent exhibitions (*above*). General Tom Thumb (*right*) was one of his greatest successes.

In 1871, he opened a circus, "The Greatest Show on Earth," and sent it out to barnstorm the nation. The combination of Barnum and Bailey came ten years later.

P. T. BARNUM'S
New and Only Greatest Show on Earth.

IN WATER-PROOF TENTS, COVERING SEVERAL ACRES. $1,000,000 INVESTED.

A GREAT AND AMUSING ACADEMY OF OBJECT TEACHING.

Museum, Menagerie, Circus, and Hippodrome.

Will travel by rail, on 100 Steel Cars of its own, passing through New York, the Canadas, Michigan, Illinois, Minnesota, Wisconsin, Indiana, Iowa, Missouri, and Texas. The Museum contains 100,000 rare and startling curiosities, including the most remarkable Captain COSTENTENUS, a Greek nobleman, who was

TATTOED FROM HEAD TO FOOT

in Chinese Tartary, as punishment for engaging in rebellion against the King.

The **MENAGERIE** consists of by far the largest collection of living wild animals that ever travelled, among which are the $25,000 Hippopotamus from the river Nile, Sea Lions from Alaska, Giraffes, the African Lioness and her little royal Cubs, no larger than cats, a picture of which occupies a full page in HARPER'S WEEKLY of April 28th. The six beautiful jet-black $30,000 Trakene Stallions, from Paris, present amazing and ENTIRELY NOVEL performances, which have been witnessed with delight by over 200,000 ladies, gentlemen, and children this spring at Barnum's great Hippodrome Building in New York. This picture shows them

EXACTLY AS THEY APPEAR IN THE RING,

where also will appear twice each day one hundred peerless performers, funny clowns, and more than a hundred beautiful Arabian horses, ponies, elephants, camels, and other marvelously-educated performing animals. A Golden Street Procession a mile in length, full of startling features, with immense glittering Chariots, men in Armor, Bands of Music, curious Automatons, OPEN CAGES OF LIONS, in which AN INTREPID LADY PERFORMER APPEARS, and ENORMOUS SERPENTS, with their FEARLESS KEEPERS INSIDE THE CAGES, takes place daily from 9 to 10 o'clock A.M.

Cheap excursion trains, conveying passengers to the town where the exhibition takes place.

MUSICAL ARTS

AMERICAN music was as stratified as a wedding cake from 1865 to 1900. On the lowest level lay the rich ballads trolled out in barbershop harmony, the ones which celebrated mother, the fate of a wayward girl, or humble yearning for the love of a good woman. On a higher, but still masculine plane, lay the brassy marches of John Philip Sousa.

Light opera occupied the middle ground. Gilbert and Sullivan were smash hits in the United States. In 1881, five companies played *Pinafore* in New York City at the same time. Lillian Russell, a shapely beauty, began her long career by spoofing the English satirists. Big-city symphonies and music festivals brought the finest European works to America. At the top, for scale and grandeur, was the Metropolitan Opera Company. Under its aegis, the palatial Metropolitan Opera House (*left*) opened in New York with Gounod's *Faust* on October 22, 1883. Leopold Damrosch and Anton Seidl made it world famous.

American opera lovers jamming the new Metropolitan heaped adulation on such native stars as the beautiful Emma Eames (*above, left*) and singers from abroad like Australian-born Nellie Melba (*above, right*). German operas such as *Siegfried* (*below*) appeared.

219

A KIND of musical giantism existed in Victorian days. Great choral societies joined with symphony orchestras for massive presentations. Such was the Musical Festival at the Seventh Regiment Armory in New York during 1881 (*above*). In the next decade, Ocean Grove, New Jersey, produced similar concerts (*right*).

Oratorio societies drew men and women from far and near. The New York concert pictured brought singers from Brooklyn, New Jersey, and the Hudson Valley towns to make up the chorus of 1,200. A 250-man orchestra, a mighty organ, and four bands of brass instruments completed the ensemble. The enormous Berlioz *Requiem* was the featured work.

Large-scale festivals included a five-day concert in 1869, to celebrate the end of the Civil War, and a similar effort in 1872. Worcester, Massachusetts, began its annual festival in 1871; Cincinnati in 1873; and Ann Arbor, Michigan, in 1893.

220

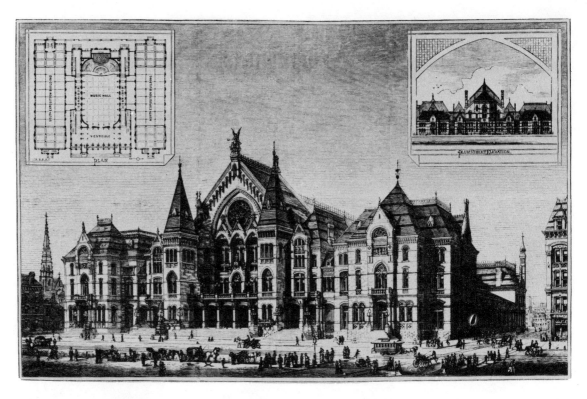

DEDICATED men, many of European background, helped feed and improve America's musical taste. Among them was the young Walter Damrosch (*left*), who took up the baton at the Metropolitan Opera in 1885 when his brilliant father died, and finished the season. He later organized his own touring opera company, and subsequently became conductor of the New York Symphony.

Another innovator was Theodore Thomas, who toured the nation with his own orchestra; went to the Cincinnati College of Music as director; conducted the New York Philharmonic and the Chicago Orchestra. He introduced the works of Wagner, Brahms, and Richard Strauss.

The Cincinnati Music Hall, a monument to the Victorian Gothic (*above*), exemplified that mellow town's high regard for the musical arts.

Progress and Growth

IMMIGRATION

Eager New Citizens by the Million Poured Into the United States in Search of the Promised Land

Until the 1890s, when Ellis Island was used, Castle Garden (*above*) in downtown New York served as the port of entry for immigrants. Frightened and bewildered, dressed as they had been in the old country (*below*), they poured ashore timidly to face registry clerks.

A PULSING tide of immigration flooded America's shores in the seventies, eighties, and nineties and continued past the turn of the century. Steerage passengers catching their first glimpse of that statue which meant America (pages 224-225) were leaving their homelands for a variety of reasons.

Religious persecution, famine, fear of compulsory military service, poverty, and the drive toward freedom and improved economic status contributed to the mass migrations. The foreign strangers were welcomed to our shores in the period immediately following the Civil War. Steamship companies beat the drum through European cities to get passengers. The great railroads, with acres of government-given land to sell, called for farmers. Industrialists, to populate their factories, made labor contracts overseas. The foreign-born

proved ideal for their new bosses. They worked for lower wages than native Americans, and because of their language difficulties, were largely deaf to the arguments of labor unions.

From 1865 to 1900, more than 13 million foreigners entered the United States. The total in the 1870-1880 decade almost reached 3 million but was held down by dismal economic conditions following the Panic of 1873, which scared off potential immigrants. The roaring eighties saw more than 5 million people pour off ships, and the next decade welcomed over 3½ million. As the great steamships docked, a horde of swindlers, con men, and sharpers fell on the innocent newcomers ·(below) with a variety of ingenious schemes designed to milk them of their slim capital. The "greenies," as they were christened, often served as dupes.

228

Some Newcomers Sought the Open Skies of the West
While Others Huddled Together in Big-city Slums

THERE was a great, sweeping change in the national origins of America's immigrants just previous to 1900. The new citizens, both before and just after the Civil War, came from northern and western Europe: England, Ireland, Germany, and Scandinavia. By the eighties and nineties, people from the South and East gained ascendancy and the liners carried a multitude of Russians, Greeks, Turks, Italians, and inhabitants of middle Europe.

The Nordic peoples—Germans, Danes, Swedes, and Norwegians—went west to populate Minnesota, Wisconsin, Kansas, Dakota Territory, Missouri, and Nebraska. Many became farmers; others worked as migrant field hands, traveling with the agricultural machinery at harvest time (*below*).

City immigrants of the newer strain established their own racial sections like Little Syria (*left*) or Chinatown (*lower left.*)

TRANSPORTATION

ONE OF the most impressive phenomena of nineteenth-century America was the steady growth of the nation's transportation system. Spectacular strides were made in railroading. Track construction across the hot plains and through narrow mountain passes made an American saga.

Completion of the first transcontinental system was the classic achievement. During the Civil War, the Union Pacific was pushed west from Omaha, and the Central Pacific, aided by the work of ten thousand Chinese coolies, drove east from Sacramento. On May 10, 1869, the lines met at Promontory Point, Utah. "Engine No. 119 from the Atlantic, and Jupiter, No. 60, from the Pacific, each decorated with flags and evergreens for the occasion, . . . approached within a hundred feet from opposite directions, and saluted with exultant screams." A gold spike to complete the construction, and a libation of champagne, celebrated the day of victory.

Construction trains, like that of the Northern Pacific (*below*), soon became part of the western picture. They carried hard-working, roughhousing crews who lived on game brought in by hired hunters like "Buffalo Bill" Cody. Such men laid iron for the Southern Pacific, the Missouri Pacific, the Kansas Pacific, and the Atchison, Topeka and Santa Fe. Broad backs and brawny shoulders put down track through such awesome country as Las Animas Cañon, in the Rocky Mountains, on the Denver and Rio Grande Railway (pages 230-231).

The Sixties and Seventies Saw an Outburst of Railroad Growth and Construction Never Equaled in the World

Violent snowstorms on the western prairies became one of railroading's worst hazards, for trains could be isolated for days because of heavy drifts. Rotary snowplows, such as this one on the Central Pacific, were pushed by several locomotives in tandem to tackle drifts.

ARLY American railway cars gave a deceptive air of spaciousness (*above*) but were drafty affairs, warmed by the fickle heat of a cast-iron stove. Improvement was rapid. By 1875, the pure in heart aboard a "Pullman Palace" car could mark their Sunday with musical services (*right*). In the 1890s, those who paid a 10 per cent extra fare to ride such trains as the "Chicago Limited" could imbibe freely in luxurious surroundings (*opposite page, top*).

George M. Pullman improved the lot of the traveler by train. The cars he turned out in Chicago ran more smoothly than their predecessors, were ornately furnished, and catered to creature comforts. Berth-equipped sleeping cars, dining cars, and provisions for private compartments all pleased increasing numbers of passengers of both sexes.

234

The Level of Comfort for Railroad Passengers Showed Improvement Throughout the Eighties and Nineties

Along with passenger comfort, speed became a fetish on the railroads, especially on "fast mail" trains which carried the government pouches between large cities. Pulling one such train, on the run from Syracuse to Buffalo, was the New York Central's Engine No. 110 (*below*) which, upon occasion, reached seventy-five miles per hour for short distances.

236

To Those with Wealth, Fast Transatlantic Travel Was Becoming a Commonplace by the Turn of the Century

STEAMER DAY" in New York brought groups of relatives to piers to wave farewell (*left*) to the lucky passengers who would soon be promenading on the wide decks of such steamers as the Inman Line's *City of New York* (*below*).

Victorian journalists loved the phrase "greyhounds of the sea." The expression was apt enough in the 1880s when racing fever struck British, German, French, and American steamship companies. Each new vessel created for Cunard, White Star, Inman, Guion, Hamburg-American, North German Lloyd's, or the Compagnie Générale Transatlantique was a "dark horse,"

seeking to set a new transatlantic speed record.

The ill-fated *Oregon* (pages 144-145) once held the crown, for a passage of six days, eight hours, and twenty-two minutes. The fastest ships usually made the passage in something less than seven days, burning a wasteful amount of coal in the process.

These Atlantic queens averaged between seven and ten thousand tons, and most were fondly believed to be unsinkable. First-class passengers lived luxuriously and those in second class were well treated. Bow and stern space, on the western run, were reserved for immigrants.

As cities mushroomed in size, public transportation became an increasingly serious problem. Horsecars caused stubborn traffic jams. New York pioneered in construction of elevated railways (*below*), which dropped hot ashes, and frightened horses. San Francisco developed the cable car, which soon moved to Chicago (*above*) and the Eastern Seaboard.

In Victorian Days, the Gentry Owned Swash Carriages
While Poorer Folk Used Bicycles for Transport

INVENTIONS

INCANDESCENT LIGHT.

IN AN era of great inventors, Thomas Alva Edison was one of the high priests. A tinkerer, an improver, a tireless experimenter, he tamed electric light and brought it into the American living room through his efficient and economical incandescent bulb.

Electric power had been used successfully by Charles F. Brush of Cleveland in his arc lights which illuminated the streets of cities (*right*). An efficient dynamo made such lighting possible and it dispelled dark corners and made thoroughfares safer and more attractive than in the past, when they were lit by gaslight. But arc lights flickered badly, produced a shockingly bright illumination, and proved expensive—all of which eliminated them for home use.

Seeking a softer, more diffused source of light for domestic purposes, Edison first planned a power system, then perfected a bulb in which a filament burned within a vacuum globe. Carbonized thread made up the first filaments, but bamboo fiber was substituted later. When the experiments proved successful, the inventor created dynamos, wiring systems, and meters, and worked to bring down the cost of his lamps. His incandescent lamp patent was granted in 1880; when he had perfected the invention to his satisfaction, he sold out.

Edison's invention created a utility business, one that was soon to come up against the ideas of the brilliant George Westinghouse. Edison was backing direct current as a power source; Westinghouse favored alternating current. Both sides sold their wares to the public, backed by convincing claims.

Consumers, in the meantime, marveled at the idea of home electric light: "As we enter the hall, we turn a switch close at hand, and immediately the hall is lighted; another switch placed in a convenient position at the parlor door controls the chandelier." It seemed too good to be true.

OHIO-BORN, Edison was a practical genius who held over 1,300 patents. He had three months of school. Starting as a newsboy, he became a telegrapher and soon improved telegraph systems, making possible the sending of four messages simultaneously. He also built a better form of stock ticker. When he invented a carbon transmitter for the telephone, he brought on war between the Bell Telephone Company and Western Union.

Many of Edison's creations were variations of existing machines; the phonograph was his own invention. After wrapping a piece of tinfoil around a cylinder, he talked into a diaphragm connected with a stylus which marked the vibrations on the foil. Another diaphragm-stylus combination picked up from the track and sent back sound waves from the recording. The invention was patented in 1878; shortly, Edison was talking into an improved model (*above*). Alexander Graham Bell further improved the machine, and Emile Berliner created the circular record.

Arranging a series of still pictures to give the semblance of motion intrigued many men in the late nineteenth century, Edison among them. Borrowing George Eastman's celluloid roll film, the "Wizard of Menlo Park" invented a camera called the Kinetograph and a projector called the Kinetoscope. With them, such explosive phenomena as a sneeze (*right*) could be documented. The Kinetoscope was marketed in 1893 and became popular at penny arcades, for single viewing.

Others brought motion pictures to perfection, but Edison saw well into the future as he worked on synchronizing photography with the phonograph in his laboratory called the Kinetographic Theater (*upper right*).

242

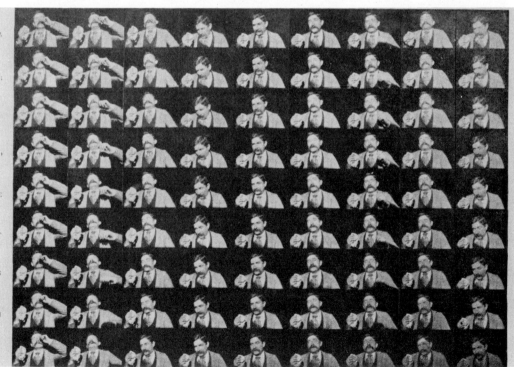

243

THE WONDERS of electricity led to a
rapid improvement in communications, as well as tremendous innovations
in the transmission of messages.

A project which came to a successful
conclusion after a series of heartbreaking failures was the opening of the
Atlantic cable connecting Europe and
America. American Cyrus W. Field
(page 169) came out of retirement to
mastermind the venture, one which was
to plague him for years. When problems
of insulation and laying techniques
were solved, the first attempt to put
down the cable took place in 1855, on
the America-Newfoundland leg, and
failed. New capital was raised as other

efforts came to nought. America was
linked to Newfoundland, but the link
from there to Ireland was a difficult one
to create. Success finally crowned Field's
efforts in 1858, but transmission soon
ceased.

In 1865, the huge *Great Eastern*
(*above*) tried again but the cable parted
at sea. The following year she succeeded
with a new line, and managed to pick up
the line lost the year before. Two lines
joined the Old and New Worlds.

Scotland gave the United States Alexander Graham Bell (*upper right*), a tall,
romantic young man who came from a
family of speech experts. After careful
training, by his family and formal

244

Both the Transatlantic Cable and the Telephone Came
In the Late 1800s to Revolutionize Business Methods

schools, Bell worked in the field of acoustics and, upon entering America, taught at the Boston School for the Deaf.

In 1875, as Bell experimented on a system to send multiple messages over one telegraph wire, the principle of the telephone came to him: a system whereby a vibrating diaphragm induced vibrations in an electromagnet, the vibrations to be carried by wire to a receiving system. The telephone was patented in 1876, in time for the Philadelphia Centennial, and primitive instruments were tested by scientists and reporters, among others (*below*).

Dubbed the "lovers' telegraph," the telephone had a meteoric rise and there were more than one and a half million instruments in the United States by 1900.

A Flood of American Inventions Gave Meaning to the Cliché "Yankee Ingenuity" as the Century Ended

SCIENTIFIC and popular publications ran occasional roundups featuring the work of American inventors (*right*). Among these was the versatile George Westinghouse (*left, with wife*) whose inventions and production methods made him a successful manufacturer at twenty-three.

Westinghouse built a small rotary engine at nineteen, then went on to create the railroad air brake and an automatic signal system to help the railways operate speedily and safely. He entered the natural gas business, creating safety valves, a transmission system, and a gas meter. The Pittsburgh innovator made alternating current practical by improvements on a transformer, and pioneered in turbine and hydroelectric power systems.

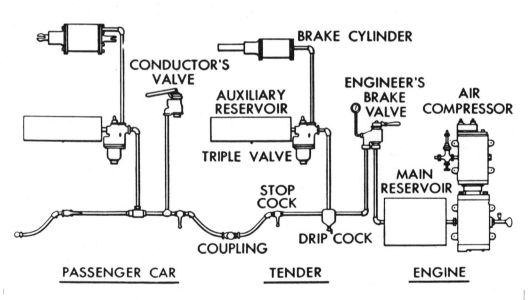

The Westinghouse air brake system shown above has built-in safety factors for situations beyond normal operation. Each car has its own reservoir of compressed air. If, for any reason, cars should break away from a train, a drop in pressure automatically applies the brakes. Better brakes made possible faster passenger trains than before, and longer freight trains to haul big pay loads. With money made from his air brakes, Westinghouse organized or financed more than sixty companies. The inventor received at least 361 patents.

REVIEW OF RECENT INVENTIONS.
By EDWARD H. KNIGHT.
[Second Article.]

THERE is a fashion in invention; not a change founded upon mere vagaries, but *tempora mutantur, et nos mutamur in illis*. New needs occur, and a hundred men volunteer for the occasion. When the civil war broke out in 1861, the ingenious mind of the people could not rest easy while muzzle-loading muskets were served out to the soldiers. A few breech-loading rifles were then in use, principally of the Maynard and Sharps patterns, but not one man in ten in the United States had ever seen a breech-loading fire-arm. Even the chamber of the revolver was then loaded from the forward end. No simple mechanical problem has ever received so many solutions as that of the breech-loader. Required, a means of unclosing the rear of a gun-barrel, introducing a cartridge thereat, closing the breech, and firing the charge. The solutions of the problem that have been given have such variations in detail that about one thousand patents have been granted therefor. So of other new needs and opportunities.

PETROLEUM.—There was a time when the Seneca Indians gathered from the surface of the water in certain parts of New York and Pennsylvania a bituminous oil of peculiar smell, and with a reputation for great medicinal virtue. This Seneca-oil, rock-oil, or *petroleum*, whose Latinized name has, contrary to the usual fortune in such cases, been adopted, has been known for thousands of years in some parts of the world, the burning springs having had a reputation for sanctity, especially those of Baku, on the banks of the Caspian Sea. It was reserved, however, for the pale-faces to make a world-wide commercial success of this product of the natural distillation of carbon. An allied hydrocarbon, the naphtha of coal-tar, had been the subject of experiment for thirty years before the discovery in this country of petroleum in merchantable quantity for illuminating purposes. The coal-oil lamp was, however, no new thing. Pliny, who died from exposure to the mephitic gases at a great eruption of Vesuvius A.D. 79, describes the collection of a bituminous oil from the surface of a spring at Agrigentum (now Girgenti, the principal sea-port in Sicily for the shipment of sulphur), and its use in lamps and for the cure of the itch-scab on beasts of burden. In Crawford's *Embassy to Ava*, published in 1826, the petroleum wells are described as supplying lamp-oil for the whole Burman empire.

James Young, of Glasgow, in 1847 refined a mineral oil found in a coal mine in Derbyshire, England, and when that supply was exhausted, commenced the distillation of a bituminous shale. He pursued the business very successfully; a refinery, operating under his patent, was established in New York, and the business gradually spread as the demand increased. This directed attention to the precarious supplies obtained in the waters of Western Pennsylvania, and in 1859 Mr. Drake, of Titusville, amidst the jeers of the neighbors, bored for oil. It is said that he gave out that he was boring for brine, in order that he might not be considered as hopelessly insane. The result surprised the world, created a commerce and various industries, raised towns in Venango and Crawford counties, Pennsylvania, and depressed New Bedford and the whaling interest, superseded Cincinnati lard-oil for burning, and to a large extent sperm for lubricating.

Out of the necessities of this new business came various plans for boring and tubing the wells, which sometimes reached a depth of 600 to 1000 feet. When the well overflowed, so much the better, but otherwise pumps were inserted. The new conditions of a very small bore and great depth might seem to have sufficiently complicated the problem, but this was by no means the end of the matter. The oil at the bottom, or elsewhere in the shaft, must be isolated from the water which permeates the various seams and rifts crossed by the borer. Packing of flaxseed in bags or of expansible rubber blocks was introduced above the point where the oil flowed from the fissures in the sand-stone. The skill with which these matters were conducted is something marvelous. A man having bored a thousand feet into mother earth and tapped a hundred springs, now essays to isolate an oil-yielding portion of the vertical shaft from other portions, and lower a pump into said section; and he does it. When gas, as is not uncommon, exists in large quantities, its pressure, on emergence from the crannies of the rock, is used to drive the oil to the surface, as in Fig. 33. A packer is placed at the end of the casing, so that no space is left to allow the gas to separate from the oil. The gas, by its tendency to expand, carries with it the oil up the flowing tube, the diameter of which is proportioned to the capacity of the well.—*M'Curdy.*

Various forms of boring machines are used in sinking these deep shafts. A tubing is generally driven until the rock is reached, and then the boring commences in earnest. The plan adopted a thousand or two years ago in China in boring for brine is found effective here. The heavy drill is alternately lifted and dropped, the suspension rope being let out from time to time as the drill sinks, or a new section is added to the drill rod. At frequent intervals the drill is withdrawn, and the detritus lifted by a cylindrical shell with a valve at the bottom, and known as a sand pump.

When it becomes necessary to bore the hole evenly to receive its tubing or to enlarge at a certain place, a reamer is employed with expanding cutters, as in Fig. 34.—*Sjprell.*

Thousands of these wells have been sunk from time to time, but in all cases they appear to drain but a limited area of the oil-bearing stratum.

A means of increasing or restoring the productiveness of oil wells was invented by Colonel Roberts. It is shown in Fig. 35, and consists in exploding gunpowder or nitro-glycerine at or near the oil-bearing point, so as to increase the size of the fissures, and open new crannies into pockets of oil or bodies of rock not exhausted.

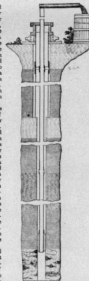

Fig. 33.—OIL WELL.

Fig. 34.—REAMING BORER.

Fig. 35.—ROBERT'S OIL-WELL.

gobien sulphuret of antimony, flowers of sulphur, starch, and water.—*Schneider.*

EXPLOSIVE COMPOUND.—Chlorate of potash, prussiate of potash or charcoal, and red phosphorus.—*Milbank.*

CONSTRUCTION OF BUILDINGS.—Whatever may be the need for pure air within-doors of healthy people in a state of freedom, the case is still more urgent with those who have no remission, but are confined in hospitals, asylums, and penitentiaries. The schools, churches, theatres, courts, and legislative halls of the land are a reproach to an enlightened community, but these are usually occupied for a few hours only of each day.

JAIL VENTILATION.—In Fig. 36 two ranges of cells constitute an interior structure, surrounded by a guard-room, which extends throughout the length and height of the building. Outer air is admitted into vaults, where it is heated, thence passes to the guard-room, through each cell in each tier, into a double corridor occupying the space between the ranges of cells, and thence into the upcast shaft or chimney.—*Mullett.*

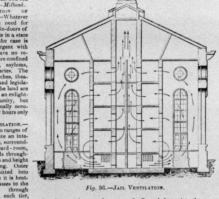

Fig. 36.—JAIL VENTILATION.

Fig. 37 is a fire-proof Mansard-roof, with a frame-work of wrought iron, having a series of knees riveted to the ends for the support of the bricks. Wires for securing the slats are passed through the joints of the brick-work, and held by iron pins.—*Conolly.*

A screen or apron of asbestos cloth, employed as a protection of buildings or other property from fire.—*Babson and Mulford.*

ARTIFICIAL STONE.—Sand, gravel, and cement, mixed with baryta, glycerine, and lime-water.—*Hall and Salisbury.*

Gravel, sand, hydraulic lime, granular waste iron, and water.—*Bérard.*

Hydraulic cement, lime powder, sugar, silicate of soda, sand, and gravel.—*Colby and Evans.*

MORTAR. COMPOSITION FOR HARDENING.—Nitrate of potash or soda, sugar, lime, mortar, and cement. Or, nitrate of potash, sugar, hyposulphite and silicate of soda.—*Colby.*

CEMENT FOR STOVE LINING.—Native fire-clay, mixed with burned and powdered fire-brick, and moulded.—*Witherell.*

PAVING.—Tar, 100; sulphuric acid, 1; linseed-oil, 3; lime to saturation: when used, it is melted and mixed with sand or sawdust.—*Porter.*

ROOFING.—Asbestos as a binding material in cements, mortars, and mastics.—*Johns.*

ROOFING AND PAVING TILE.—Silica, sulphate of lime, hydraulic lime, sulphate of potassa, alum, borax, sulphuric acid, and carbonic acid.

A hollow corrugated iron column or girder (Fig. 38), having a core which stiffens the pillar and prevents collapse.—*Manes.*

FIRE-ESCAPE.—A ladder (Fig. 39) in sections, which are raised to an inclined position by a cogged roller, which engages with an adjustable rack. The sections are then extended telescopically by means of ropes and a winch upon the carriage.—*Davis.*

WIRE ROPE.—A wire rope made up of wires each of which has an equal taper at all parts of its length, each wire being continuous throughout the whole length of the rope.—*Roebling.*

CARPET LINING.—Composed of flattened paper tubes or cases, with fillings of cotton batting laid side by side and connected by binding strips. Pressure rolls, and two endless aprons provided with transverse ribs, serve to press together and carry along the binding tapes, and flattened rolls made of batting inclosed in paper, the tapes being first carried over pasting cylinders. Steam-pipes for drying are arranged between the sets of pressure rolls and on both sides of the lining.—*Mayall.*

RAILWAY CAR SPRINGS.—Fig. 40 is a spiral metallic car spring, made from a flat bar of steel, and having coils with broad flat surfaces decreasing in diameter from each end, whereby the coils are prevented from telescoping.—*Hansell.*

Fig. 41 is a coiled spring of half-round bars, solid or grooved, and variously associated; in apposition to form a tube, or placed co-axially in duplicate or triplicate.—*Clooney.*

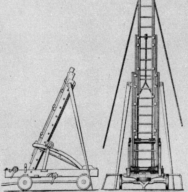

Fig. 37.—FIRE-PROOF MANSARD-ROOF.

Fig. 38.—CORRUGATED IRON COLUMN WITH CORE.

Fig. 39.—FIRE-ESCAPE LADDER.

Automatic production of the written word owed much to nineteenth-century inventions such as the typewriter, created by Christopher L. Sholes (*above, left*), Carlos Glidden and S. W. Soule. Philo Remington bought the idea and was soon turning out machines like the one shown above at right, decorated with enameled flowers and mother-of-pearl. On a different scale were the big presses like Hoe's "Web Printing Machine" as shown below.

The Last Frontier

INDIANS

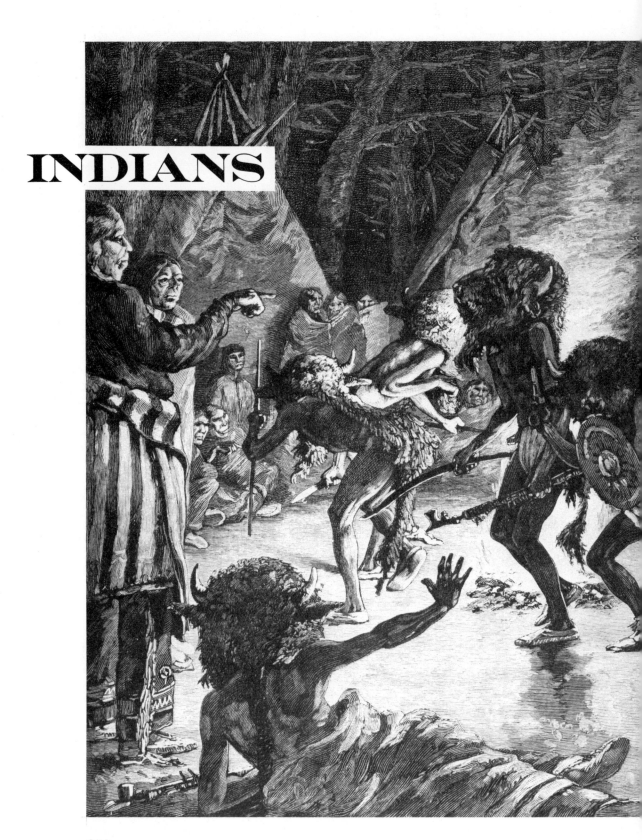

Because they were on the move following the buffalo (*above*), Plains Indians used tepees, or conical skin shelters, as homes. They were easily dismantled. Ponies dragged the poles; outside skins were made into bundles and pulled on frames called *travois* by dogs or horses. Logs helped insulate against winter blasts (*below*) when tribes settled for the season.

The Horsemen of the Great Midcontinent Became the Best Known of All America's Primitive Inhabitants

LEAN and hard, with copper skins and the panther's grace, the Plains Indians fought the white man tooth and nail and wove a place for themselves in the fabric of American history.

They were latecomers in the American culture picture, following more established eastern and southern peoples like the Iroquois and Cherokees. With a few exceptions, red men of the flat country were "bad Indians" to the U.S. infantry and cavalry who faced their rifles, bows, and tomahawks.

Plains Indians existed by hunting and fishing. The horse and the buffalo were mainstays. Descended from escaped horses of the Spanish conquerors, the Indian ponies proved tough, hardy, and fleet. They could wheel in a tight circle, freeze as their masters fired, or stretch out for long runs over the flats.

Buffaloes fed, clothed, and warmed the Indians. Their flesh was tasteful and nourishing. Tanned hides made robes to keep out the chill wind over the plains. Their dried dung provided fuel.

Indians were nomads, restless and constantly on the move. They followed the trail of the great humped beasts which provided their livelihood, and their camping spots were determined by weather and water supply.

Warfare ranked with buffalo hunting, for sport and glory. There was little organized, large-scale combat, but series of raids for horse stealing or collecting enemy scalps. Warriors painted their faces, and wore elaborate feathered headdresses for ceremonials.

About 225,000 Plains Indians existed in 1865; among the great tribes were the Sioux, Arapahoe, Blackfoot, Ute, and Apache. Representing other important peoples are (*left, top to bottom*) a Kiowa, a Cheyenne, and a Comanche.

253

Hunting ceremonies like the buffalo dance (pages 250-251) were common to plains tribes. The ghost dance of the Sioux (*above*) was a religious ritual, based on a messiah. Such rituals brought on the Battle of Wounded Knee. Most war parties did not need such rites to inspire their raids on cowboys (*below*), stagecoaches, and wagon trains (*opposite page*).

The Indian Temperament Was Unstable and Frequent Celebration of Religious Ceremonies Often Led to Battle

Manning Frontier Garrisons

VIOLENT Indian outbreaks occurred during the Civil War and afterwards, and sporadic fighting continued until the 1890s. The red men had many things to protest. Most important was the destruction of the buffalo, on which they depended for existence.

The huge, docile beasts were slaughtered by millions (pages 270-271) at the hands of the white man. As the railroads pushed west, professional hunters cut down buffalo to feed the workers.

The great westward push of the nineteenth century brought direct competition between the Indian and white man for land. Ranchers, homesteaders and miners pushed into Indian territory, laying claim to huge tracts, often in direct violation of treaties made between the Indians and the U.S. government. When his protests were in vain, the Indian took to the warpath.

The nation called on the U. S. Army to protect settlers, police the West, and

Hard-riding cavalrymen (*below*) were the elite of the Indian-fighting soldiers by reason of their horses and their triple armament of carbine, saber, and pistol. In critical moments, specified troops members took charge of the horses, and the cavalry fought dismounted.

In the Days of Indian Uprisings Was a Real Man's Job

end the Indian menace. Under Chief of Staff William T. Sherman in Washington, some 25,000 troops worked at the difficult task.

Civil War leaders led the troops. "Little Phil" Sheridan saw western service, as did Winfield S. Hancock and Alfred H. Terry. Brigadier General Edward R. S. Canby met death at the hands of an Indian named Captain Jack during the Modoc War.

Army life on the frontier was hard. The small garrisons—Forts Laramie, Connor, Phil Kearny, C. F. Smith, Wallace, Sill and others—had few comforts and no facilities for recreation. Hunting and fishing to provide antelope or trout as a welcome substitute for bacon and beans brought relief from the monotony of camp life.

Garrison life was heaven when compared with active campaigning. The long blue lines crossing vast plains areas on the track of Indians met the aching glare of sunlight or the wind-whipped blizzards which cut and stung their faces and penetrated to their bones. Until fur caps and coats were issued, ordinary soldiers met the icy blasts in regular uniforms.

At the end of the trail, death often waited for the footsore soldiers. Such was the case for the men of the Seventh Cavalry who accompanied Lieutenant Colonel George Armstrong Custer (*opposite page*) to the Little Big Horn River in Montana Territory on June 25, 1876. Custer, a flamboyant leader who had been brevetted major general, was operating in a campaign against the Sioux. He had always taken chances; on that June day he split his force in three parts, and personally led a section of over two hundred men into an ambush of waiting Indians under Sitting Bull. Not a soldier survived. Custer's poor judgment gave him a place in American history.

Blue-clad, foot-slogging infantry tramped their weary way across western deserts and sought cover wherever they could when bands of mounted Indians attacked. Civil War veterans from both sides, some regular Army men, and immigrants swelled the ranks.

Battles with the Indians for Possession of the West
Lasted Some 25 Years After the End of the Civil War

The Battle of Birch Creek, which took place August 17, 1878, in eastern Oregon, was typical of the engagements making up the Indian troubles of the post-Civil War period. Dug in among lava rocks, the enemy forced army cavalry and infantry to make an uphill fight. Soldiers made three charges, of short duration, before the Indians faded away. Army losses totaled five enlisted men wounded and 20 horses killed battling the foe.

THE BATTLE between the U. S. Army and the "horse Indians" was a long, drawn-out affair of small skirmishes and engagements. The Platte Bridge battle, encounters on the Powder and Washita Rivers, Beecher's Island, engagements on the Staked Plains, the Apache War were all small in scale when compared to the mass murder of the Civil War.

Crazy Horse's ambush, which sent two thousand Cheyennes, Sioux, and Arapahoes against a small detachment near Fort Phil Kearny, Dakota Territory, on December 21, 1866, brought on a sharp battle (below). U.S. casualties were eighty-two and the Indians lost about sixty. During the Black Hills cam-paign against the Sioux and Cheyenne in 1876, the Battle of the Rosebud River resulted in ten killed and thirty-four wounded for the troops in blue.

Nevertheless, a man killed in a skirmish was just as dead as one killed in a battle. The Indians were crafty and elusive fighters and their hit-and-run tactics were those of irregular cavalry and guerilla fighters. The savages of the plains showed themselves to be magnificent horsemen and they adapted quickly to use of the rifle.

Occasionally the Indians holed up for stubborn fighting. The Modocs, in northern California, maintained their positions in the lava beds, through storms of fire, for portions of 1872-73.

259

Army Leaders Battled a Group of Influential Chieftains

High in the ranks of redoubtable Indian fighters were Brigadier General George Crook (*left*) and Colonel Nelson Miles (*right*). Crook fought the Sioux in 1876, then went to Arizona to battle the Apache, forcing surrender of Geronimo. Breaking out, the Apache chief eventually yielded to Miles, who also captured Chief Joseph, an influential man.

THE INDIANS' battle to halt migration to the West was futile. There was a certain amount of justice in their efforts. The United States did not cover itself with glory in dealing with its primitives.

Treating the tribes as sovereign nations, the government promised certain of their lands would be inviolate. But the rush of emigration and the chance of quick riches through mining strikes led whites to invade Indian lands. As Indians were given poorer and poorer territory, they revolted.

Attempts were made to provide sufficient living space for all Indians in reservations, especially in the land known as Indian Territory, which is now Oklahoma. Reservation life meant grants of food such as cattle, which the red men hunted down and butchered themselves (*right*), and promises of education for Indian children. But free-roaming nomads found the idleness restrictive and the Sioux, Cheyenne, Arapahoe, and Apache people broke loose when they could. The Bureau of Indian Affairs, responsible for the savages, was riddled with corrupt and venal men.

In 1871, the government stopped making useless treaties with the chiefs and took the Indians under its wing as national wards. Reservations filled up. A measure of Indian independence came with the Dawes Severalty Act of 1887. Under it, the president could end tribal government in any reservation and distribute the land among individual Indians, who acquired citizenship with the land grants.

Who Were Confused by U.S. Government Policies

Joseph (*left*), one of the supreme Indian leaders, captained his Nez Percé people of the Northwest in a magnificent fighting retreat from the attacking U. S. Army. Geronimo (*right*) was the wily chief of an Apache band who escaped into Mexico and led a series of bloody raids on Arizona. Captured by Miles in 1886, he dictated his autobiography.

EMIGRATION

263

Railroads and Wagon Trains Carried Settlers from
The Sedate East to the Vast Plains of the New West

ETWEEN 1865 and 1890, the American frontier disappeared. Homesteaders, ranchers, miners, men who would become itinerant harvesters and fruit pickers, all headed for the lands beyond the Missouri. From 1860 to 1880, seven million people poured into the West.

The rapid rise of the railroads, and special trains for emigrants, attracted many new settlers. The Union Pacific Railroad station at Omaha (*opposite page, top, and pages 262-263*) displayed a fascinating conglomerate of fortune seekers. *Crofutt's Guide* (*left*) gave valuable tips on rail travel in the 1870s.

Emigrants for sparsely settled areas took wagon trains like the one shown above making a food stop in Helena, Montana. "Bull trains" of oxen (*opposite page, left*) carried freight into newly developed lands.

265

Painted Indians and Masked Highwaymen Spiced the
Dangerous Travel Routes of West-bound Emigrants

TRAVELERS bound for the Great Plains or the fertile Pacific Coast ran risks by day and night. Those who went by buckboard or wagon, on short exploration trips, maintained a sharp watch for hostile Indians (*opposite page, top*). Stagecoach passengers grew to expect armed men who quickly rifled pockets and baggage (*opposite page, bottom*). When coaches carried gold, or pay for the army garrisons, mounted bandits became a greater menace than before.

Some of the most spectacular country in the world greeted the eyes of west-moving emigrants. In the badlands of the Little Missouri were lunar landscapes (*below*). Pioneers looking at such fertile spots as the Upper Yosemite Valley felt they had found the promised land.

For most, the going was less than ideal. A traveler to the Black Hills country in 1877 spelled out his troubles for *Scribner's Magazine:*

"Our vehicles consisted of what is commonly termed a 'jerky,' and a large freight wagon, each drawn by four horses. I believe the 'jerky' derived its name from the peculiar, not to say sportive, manner in which it switched its driver from the seat whenever any rough road was passed. The prospect of riding 300 miles on a springless wagon was not inviting. . . . Our course lay up the Platte for several miles through deep and heavy sand and the sun poured down with greater fierceness than I had ever before known . . . we were surrounded and harassed all morning by innumerable sand-gnats, which darted into our eyes, crawled into our nostrils, buzzed in our ears and wriggled down our necks . . . during the afternoon the country over which our road trailed its sinuous course grew rougher and more jagged . . . the horizon was completely hemmed in by clouds, and a drizzling rain settling in. The party has eight colds, all told. Breakfast, a swindle."

Winter sealed the fields and came down like a freezing iron hand on the bare sod houses of the West (*above*). Bitter blizzards in Montana and Dakota brought real threats to existence as they blocked off roads needed in emergencies. In summer, when prairie fires blazed, farmers plowed firebreaks to stem the flames (*below*) which threatened homes.

268

Those Families Who Settled Down to Farm the Great Plaᵢ.

THE SOLID men of the West were the homesteaders, the emigrants who sought to settle on rich farm land and raise their families. Many of those who put down roots in Kansas, Nebraska, or in the Montana and Dakota Territories came from overseas; from Germany, Sweden, Norway, Denmark, and Russia.

Railroad expansion made ready roads to the West. Slowly and painfully, the U. S. Army was eliminating Indian domination of the western plains. Procuring the land itself for settlement was no great problem. Under the Homestead Act of 1862, a settler could acquire 160 acres of ground by living on it for five years, cultivating it, and paying a small fee. The act applied to citizens, and those who declared their intentions of becoming citizens.

Land could be bought from the United States government, up to 1891, for $1.25 an acre. Land could be purchased from the states, which had been given thirty thousand acres (when they established a public agricultural college) for each representative they had in Congress, under the Morrill Act. And the railroads, holding great tracts given them as bonuses for construction, were anxious to sell. Settlers who would pay got good land for from five to ten dollars an acre from the states and railway companies.

Emigrants who settled in the territories could look forward, in most cases, to statehood before the turn of the century. In 1889, North Dakota, South Dakota, Montana, and Washington entered the Union as states. The following year saw the entrance of Idaho and Wyoming; Utah entered in 1896. Oklahoma, Arizona, and New Mexico came in after 1900.

Men and women opening up these fresh new lands had tough sledding as they struggled to make their start. Many whose wagons carried "Kansas or Bust" signs busted, and returned to their old lives in the East.

The Plains had much to give, but to achieve their bounty a man had to work hard, buck severe extremes of weather and remain indifferent to loneliness. A mailbox was often the single link to the outside world for weeks at a time (*left*). Western farms were big ones, unlike those of the East, and opportunities for socializing were lacking.

Life became especially hard for the women. The niceties—church socials, picnics, husking bees—of the East were lacking. Chores of the home and farmyard seemed never-ending. Children received much of their early education at home and carried out their full share of laborious duties.

SLAUGHTER

THE HERD LEADER.

270

ONE OF the most shameful events in American history was the senseless mass slaughter of wildlife which reached its peak between 1865 and 1900. North America may have been the greatest game refuge in the world; certainly the forests, plains, and skies were stocked with buffalo, elk, antelope, bear, beaver, mink, deer, duck, and pigeon. In the course of a generation, professional and amateur hunters, Indians, ranchers, emigrants, and sportsmen undeserving of the name had laid about them with a heavy hand and harried American wildlife almost out of existence.

Destruction of the buffalo was the classic example. Historians say the bison herds of the nation may have represented the greatest concentration of a single species ever seen. Estimates place some 60 million of the shaggy, lumbering beasts in North America when the white man came, and they ranged east as far as New York, Georgia, and the Carolinas, and wandered from Canada to the states along the Mexican border.

At the close of the Civil War, there may have been 15 million buffalo in the Great Plains area. In twenty years they were almost gone.

The railroads sounded the death knell for the bison. Driving west, they separated the buffalo into northern and southern herds. The southern herd went first; the northern herd, in rough country, lasted a little longer. Beasts that escaped the hunters moved into Canada. In the 1870s, for a period, one million animals were killed each year.

Completion of the railroads provided transportation to the East for buffalo meat and hides and the mass slaughter increased. Destruction was almost unbelievable; in many cases, only 1 per cent of the meat was shipped. The markets were soon glutted. Hides brought less than a dollar apiece. Army men and sportsmen (*below*) killed as wantonly as the hunters. By 1890, the great herds were seen no more.

The Rich and Abundant Animal Life Reported by Lewis And Clark Disappeared in the Late Nineteenth Century

White men, Indians, and sportsmen from abroad shared in destroying the great elk herds (*above*). Repeating rifles helped make the mass murder possible. Because of their tender meat and soft hides, females and half-grown animals were prime targets. Western trains, often with special hunting cars attached, brought the killers to the antelope (*right*).

272

THE PRONGHORN antelope (*below*), a beautiful and speedy animal, was almost as numerous as the buffalo on the western plains. The lumbering elk (*left*) wandered in great herds through most of North America. Both presented tempting targets for the meat hunters.

Once the railways began to haul dead animals into the Midwest and East, game became immensely popular on American tables. For a time, the demand was great and prices rose. With no regard for the future, and without the dimmest understanding of conservation, hunters plundered the herds.

Wasteful destruction became the rule. Animals were shot for a few pounds of tender meat, or for hides alone. The carcasses of beasts rotted on the plains and fed the wolves and vultures.

Indian destruction of game was as wasteful as the white man's in many cases, but the red man made better use of the animals. In addition, Indians were constantly on the move. Areas over which they hunted were soon restocked with game by natural processes.

Elk and antelope were indiscriminately killed by stockmen so they could not compete with cows and sheep for grazing land. The pronghorns were almost driven to extinction; the elk moved into the Rocky Mountains and the state of Washington.

FRENZENY & TAVERNIER

273

Nothing Clad in Fur, Feathers, or Hide Seemed Safe
From the Ravaging Hunters of the Sixties and Seventies

HOOFED animals were by no means the only ones to be decimated by hunters of the late nineteenth century. In Alaskan and Aleutian waters, and among the Pribilof Islands, fur seals existed by millions in the years after the Civil War. Destruction of the seals (*below*), and sea otters as well, by foreign nationals as well as Americans, led to international incidents.

In the Rocky Mountains, tough hunters battled bears for sport; in the garden country of California, farmers destroyed jack rabbits by thousands to prevent the rodents from destroying crops (*opposite page, lower left*).

Next to the destruction of the buffalo, the mass slaughter of bird life became the most disgraceful in a series of irresponsible events brought about by American hunters. The trophies hung from a railroad car (*left*) behind their proud killers represent one day's sport near Webster, Dakota Territory.

The blazing shotguns of men such as those shown helped drive the passenger pigeon into extinction. These beautiful birds once existed in incredible masses estimated in billions. Mass hunting brought a sharp decline in their numbers in the 1880s. The last one died in 1914.

COWBOYS

277

FROM 1865 to 1885, the "Cattle Kingdom" flourished in the West, pouring riches into the pockets of cattle barons and ensconcing the cowboy in American folklore. Vast areas between the Missouri River and the Rockies trembled to pounding hoofs as huge herds of longhorns surged northward to fresh pastures. The era was steeped in local color. Its stories and legends thrilled easterners and Europeans.

Several factors combined to make the western states the feeding grounds for millions of steers in the years after the Civil War. Most important was the existence of huge areas of public domain in the Great Plains area. Grass and water were free to all. The Indians were being driven back and the buffalo disappearing, opening enormous acreage for cattlemen to use as they pleased. Of immediate economic importance was the westward thrust of the railroads. Cattle could be loaded on cars at the new railhead towns, then shipped to the packing houses of the Midwest. The beasts were slaughtered there, then sent east in the new refrigerator cars.

The gaudy period began with the great era of the "Long Drive." Huge herds of Texas cattle were collected yearly and driven north to fatten on the pasture land there, then routed to railroad sidings for shipment. By the 1870s, hundreds of thousands of beef cattle made the annual trek.

Cowboys riding the migrating herds coming up from Texas used the Sedalia Trail which led to Sedalia, on the Missouri Pacific Railroad; the Chisholm Trail to Newton, Kansas, on the Santa Fe, or to Ellsworth and Abilene, on the Kansas Pacific; and the Western Trail to Dodge City, Kansas, another Santa Fe point. The early trails crossed Indian Territory into Kansas. As the rail lines

For Two Decades the American Cowboy Created His
Saga from the Rio Grande to the Canadian Border

moved west, so did the trails. The Goodnight-Loving Trail angled sharply west through Texas, crossed the Pecos River, then swung north through New Mexico and Colorado to intersect the Union Pacific east of Cheyenne, Wyoming.

The great cattle drives were enormous, thrilling productions. Herds numbered one thousand or more and were controlled by a handful of cowboys who kept them moving in a general northerly direction, letting them graze as they wandered. Chuck wagons accompanied the riders to feed them, and a trail boss kept order. Scouts kept their eyes peeled for hostile Indians, rustlers, and the streams necessary to water the huge concentrations of beasts. In 1866, more than a quarter million cattle came up from Texas.

Eventually the long drives slackened. The treks caused the cattle to lose weight, and they needed long fattening before they could go to market. Emigrant farmers and protesting Indians drove the migrating herds from their lands. State laws restricted the passage of cattle.

The solution was the establishment of permanent ranches in Texas, which was being penetrated by the railroads, and in the Great Plains, where Herefords and Anguses could graze on public land. Kansas, Nebraska, Colorado, as well as Wyoming and Montana Territories, became the great ranges. The great blizzard of 1886 (*left*), plus economic factors, marked the beginning of the end for the free-wheeling kind of cattle business.

The barbed-wire fence, invented in 1874, became both a curse and a blessing to the cowboy. He used it (*below*) to fence his own ranch. But emigrants, to protect their farm land, often ringed property with barbed wire to keep out the herds of cattle making the long drive.

The Excitement of Pounding the Trail, Then Celebrating

As the days of the long drives passed, cowboys found their excitement at roundup time when they were likely to be caught up in a herd of stampeding cattle (*above*). Roundups took place twice a year, in spring and fall, to cut out and brand newborn calves, and to help separate the beasts of neighboring herds sharing the public domain. Like the wheat harvests, roundups meant long and hard work but brought friends together temporarily.

Explosively in Scarlet Cities, Slackened Off in the 1880s

When ranching went respectable, the incidents which gave the railhead towns their lurid color disappeared. Cowboys on the long drive, after days of breathing alkali dust, craved liquor and created their own fracases. Brawls in bars sometimes created lasting legends.

KANSAS supported more than 1½ million cattle in 1880, and Nebraska had over one million. Surprisingly, they wintered well despite snow and blast as long as the ground was ice-free. But luck ran out between 1885 and 1887 when severe winter weather killed animals by the thousands.

The ravages of snow and ice were merely another nail in the coffin of an already staggering industry. News of huge profits to be made from beef had gone beyond western borders. Rising prices stirred the imaginations of capitalists in the East and in Europe. Syndicates were formed, capital was invested, cowboys were hired, and ranching became big business controlled by absentee owners. In the meantime, the idea of bountiful profit stirred restless easterners who railroaded west to make their fortunes.

Eventually, the saturation point was reached. The land became overgrazed and cattle could not fatten properly. Mounting costs for cattle and fear of stripped down land led ranchers into the big cattle cooperatives of the 1880s which fenced in grazing land to keep out strangers. Overproduction of beef cattle began to take its toll, and prices tumbled. With pasturage growing scarce and prices falling, the big business of ranching seemed suddenly unattractive. Men sold out, took their losses, and left the cattle business to a new breed.

Chaps, a Protective Handkerchief, a Broad Hat, a Rawhide Lariat, and a Six Gun Marked the Cowboy

THE COWBOY of the late 1880s was probably the supreme American folk hero. Wedded to his sturdy, tough mustang, an expert with the lariat, he has been fixed in time by Frederic Remington, who made the pictures on these pages.

Richard Harding Davis, writing for *Harper's Weekly*, left an accurate description: "The cowboy cannot be overestimated as a picturesque figure; all that has been written about him and all the illustrations . . . fail to spoil the picture he makes when one sees him for the first time racing across a range outlined against the sky, with his handkerchief flying out behind, his sombrero bent back by the wind, and his gauntlets and broad leather leggings showing above and at the side of his galloping pony. And his deep seat in the saddle, with his legs hanging straight to the long stirrups, the movement of his body as it sways and bends, and his utter unconsciousness of the animal beneath him, would make a German riding master, an English jockey, or the best cross-country rider of a Long Island hunting club shake his head in envy and despair.

"He is a fantastic-looking individual, and one suspects he wears the strange garments he affects because he knows they are most becoming. But there is a reason for each of the different parts of his apparel . . . the sombrero shades his face from the rain and sun, the rattlesnake-skin around it keeps it on his head, the broad kerchief that he wears knotted around his throat protects his neck from the heat, and the leather leggings which cover the front of his legs protect them from the cactus in Texas, and in the North, where the fur and hair are left on the leather, from the sleet and rain as he rides against them.

The gauntlets certainly seem too military for such rough service, but any one who has had a sheet rope run through his hands can imagine how a lasso cuts when a wild horse is pulling on the other end of it. His cartridge-belt and his revolver are on some ranches superfluous, but cattle-men say they have found that on those days when they took this toy away from their boys, they sulked and fretted and went about their work half-heartedly so that they believe it pays better to humor them. . . ."

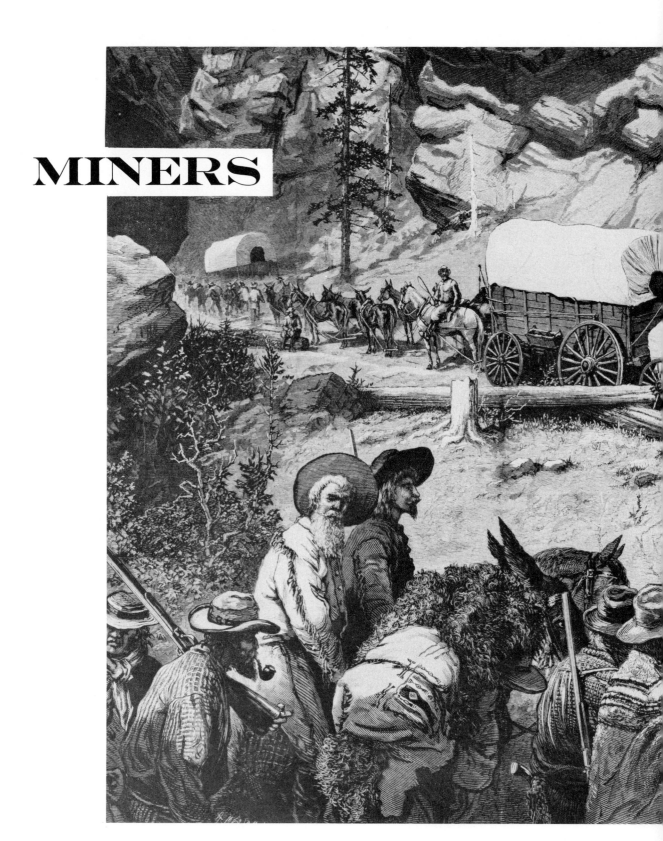

MINERS

Prospectors, Singly or in Pairs, Cut New Trails
In the West as They Carried Out an Ancient Hunt

Prospectors working the Black Hills country of Dakota came in response to persistent rumors of gold buried in the rocks of the rugged mountains. Wild and lonesome, the country belonged to the Sioux and was protected by the U. S. Army. The Indians refused to leave. Pressure on the government and the Army led to the opening of the land in 1875. Packing bedrolls, going their solitary ways, the hardy frontiersmen (*above*) took their chances.

THE LAST of the rugged frontiersmen who opened the West were the miners, a restless and independent group of individualists seeking gold and silver in the bowels of the earth. They crisscrossed the land, from the Missouri River to the Pacific, between Mexico and Canada. Their ways were rough and their habits nomadic, but they did much to organize the western territories and prepare them for statehood.

News of gold or silver was electrifying, and eager prospectors, once alerted, poured into virgin country by riverboat, railroad, covered wagon (pages 284-285), or muleback. In many cases the news was false or misleading, and the lemminglike mass migrations fizzled out.

Mining fever reached a high point during the Civil War. Californians and those from the Far West turned their backs on the conflict and grubbed for riches.

Just before the war, a gold discovery near Pike's Peak, in what was to become Colorado, drew thousands and helped create Denver and Boulder. The strike soon proved an enormous false alarm. A real find at this time was the silver of the Comstock Lode, which created Nevada Territory, established the hell-raising Virginia City, and yielded over 300 million dollars in twenty years.

The big mining strikes which in three decades produced more than 2 billion dollars in gold and silver took place in what we now know as Colorado, Nevada, Wyoming, Montana, Idaho, and Washington. California had led off with the Gold Rush of 1849; in 1874, the rush to the Black Hills of Dakota Territory marked the beginning of the end.

A lodestone for those seeking mineral riches was the Sierra Madre Mountains country of New Mexico and Mexico. For the delectation of readers in the East, Frederic Remington put down on paper two typical prospectors of the area. Heavily armed against the threat of Apache bands, the men travel with tough, tiny burros which carry bacon, flour, coffee, sugar, tobacco, and ammunition, along with picks and shovels, blankets, and cooking equipment.

Between the First Strikes and the Arrival of Eastern Capitalists, the Wild Mining Towns Had Their Day

The shift change in a Nevada silver mine shown above is indicative of the progress which overtook the prospector and numbered his days. Individuals could pan or sluice for gold, or even sink small shafts with a minimum of assistance. But when precious metals were locked in quartz more than a hundred feet down, many men, efficiently bossed, were needed to carry out mining operations. Outside capitalists moved in, and pioneers trekked on.

FRONTIER mining towns blazed with color, reveled in wickedness, and brought together hard-working prospectors, gamblers, desperadoes, flame-cheeked prostitutes, gunmen, one-time convicts as well as "men of wealth and brains, young graduates of colleges eager for a business opening, engineers and surveyors, lawyers, doctors, and a thousand soft-handed triflers who hoped to make a living in some undefined way out of the general excitement."

Crude settlements like Deadwood, in the Black Hills (*above*), were slapped together overnight. Leadville, Colorado, was made of "log huts, board shanties, canvas tents, kennels dug into the hillside and roofed with earth and pine boughs." New inhabitants "were glad to pay for the privilege of spreading their overcoats or blankets on the floor of a saloon."

In permanent towns like Denver, huge gambling houses (*right*) funneled off the profits prospectors collected from pay dirt.

In Their Search for Mineral Wealth, Prospectors Quickly Invaded the Land of the Northwest Mounted

THE TOUGHEST and hardiest adventurers sought gold in the frozen wastes of Alaska during the last years of the nineteenth century. Juneau became the outfitting point. Traveling painfully by foot, prospectors crossed snowbanked areas like the Chilkoot Pass (*left*) on their way to the mining country. A gold strike on the Seward Peninsula in 1899 created Nome.

Of greater excitement was the Klondike strike in 1896, in northwestern Canada's Yukon Territory, just east of the Alaska border. The gold rush of 1897-98 which resulted brought thousands from the United States to the settlements of Dawson and the Klondike Creek area. Sluice mining (*below*) was popular. When the "wash-up" was over for the year, leather bags holding gold were brought to banks which sometimes weighed as much as a quarter million dollars' worth of the yellow metal a day (*right*).

*Miners Cheered as the First Steamer Loaded With
Klondike Gold Left Dawson City in June, 1898*

Empire Building

WAR WITH SPAIN

CHARLES J. deLACY 1898.

294

The flashing machetes of the insurgents were familiar throughout the cane plantations of Cuba, which had long fought Spanish domination, notably in the Ten Years' War of 1868-78. After the 1895 revolt and a series of depredations, Spain sent Valeriano Weyler, nicknamed "The Butcher," to enforce order in a cruel and ruthless manner of his own.

Was to Become a Most Popular Conflict in the U.S.A.

Mahan was a "big navy" man. His most influential work, *The Influence of Sea Power upon History, 1660-1783*, was read around the world by students of war and politics.

CAPTAIN Alfred T. Mahan of the United States Navy was a vigorous proponent of naval strength. His doctrines proved influential. Americans looked with pride on such new warships as *New York* (*below*) which in the eighties and nineties were helping form a well-armed steel fleet.

The new navy played an impressive part in the brief ten-week war against Spain which filled American newspapers with derring-do in 1898.

In 1895, the Cubans had revolted against their Spanish rulers in a burst of guerilla warfare and the Spaniards retaliated savagely. U.S. reaction was strong: there were American business interests in Cuba, the big island lay just off our doorstep, and there was enormous sympathy for the native people. The mysterious sinking of the *Maine* at Havana set the press to screaming. Pushed on by public and Congressional clamor, President William McKinley sent an ultimatum to Spain, and Congress boiled over with jingoism. On April 24, Spain declared war.

Free Press

BULLETIN. BULLETIN.

ONE CENT. ONE CENT.
2:45 P. M. SEVENTH EXTRA. 2:45 P. M.

DETROIT, MICH., THURSDAY, APRIL 21, 1898

ORDERED TO CUBA!

Squadron at Key West Has Just Received Orders.

Washington, April 21.=Special.=Squadron at Key West has just been ordered to Cuba.

EXECUTE YOUR ORDERS!

This Means Blockade of Havana!

Washington, April 21.—Special.—Following telegram sent to Sampson: "Proceed to sea and execute your orders." This means blockade of Havana.

Heavy Guns of the U.S. Navy

The American public clasped Dewey to its bosom after the Manila victory. Popular songs, commemorative busts and pictures, and torrents of oratory all did honor to the man who was the hero of the hour.

Brought the U.S. Its First Victory in the War With Spain

THE AMERICAN public was tense with excitement in the week which led up to a declaration of war. Newspapers poured out streams of extras (*left*). Cuba had become the center of all eyes, and there was a fear that the Spanish fleet might train its guns on the cities of the Atlantic seaboard.

But the first major action of the war came in the faraway Pacific. There, Commodore George Dewey led the Asiatic Squadron of the U. S. Navy from Hong Kong to Manila Bay, Philippine Islands, and destroyed the Spanish fleet in the harbor. It was a glorious victory for a nation bent on punishing the Spaniards and put the United States in a holiday mood.

In February, Assistant Secretary of the Navy Theodore Roosevelt had cabled Dewey to concentrate at Hong Kong for a possible offensive against the Philippines in case of war. When war came, Secretary of the Navy John D. Long unleashed Dewey for operations against the Spanish fleet.

The commodore, completely prepared and with a force at top efficiency, made the long trip to the islands and entered Manila Bay to find the Spanish ships just south of Manila, at Cavite. In a series of runs, six American vessels pounded ten enemy ships to pieces (*lower left*). Not a single American was lost in this engagement of May 1.

Dewey blockaded Manila and an expeditionary force under Major General Wesley Merritt left San Francisco for the islands. On August 13, in a relatively bloodless operation, U.S. troops moved on Manila (*below*) and captured the city.

BOTH fleet and land action took place in the Caribbean. Elements of the North Atlantic Fleet, under Rear Admiral William T. Sampson, blockaded Cuban ports. Admiral Pascual Cervera y Topete had left the Cape Verde Islands for an unknown destination and Sampson, reasoning that the Spanish ships would refuel at San Juan, Puerto Rico, pounded the port with gunfire (pages 294-295). Cervera outwitted Sampson, and evaded the Flying Squadron under Commodore Winfield S. Schley; coaled at Curaçao and put in at the port of Santiago, Cuba, safely in late May.

Sampson blockaded the harbor. Eventually, American pressure by land on Santiago forced Cervera to leave Santiago. On July 3, his ships attempted to shoot their way out. The Spanish fleet was demolished, and Cervera rescued.

Land action in the Caribbean took place near Santiago, Cuba, and to a small extent in Puerto Rico. President McKinley had called for 200,000 volunteers, who were hastily trained and badly equipped. To open combat, an army of 17,000 went through a nightmare of embarkation difficulties as they left Port Tampa, Florida (page 293), then landed at Daiquiri, fifteen miles east of Santiago, and at nearby Siboney.

Landing operations began June 22 and Siboney was organized as the base for a drive on Santiago.

Santiago was ringed with hills and there the Spanish put up a stout defense for a short period. July 1 saw the most bitter fighting of the war as U.S. troops took El Caney, Kettle Hill, and stormed up San Juan Hill (above). Santiago was put under siege and surrendered July 17. On August 12, an armistice ended hostilities and the war was over.

Spanish Troops Were Widely Scattered and There Was No Effective Large-scale Opposition in Cuba

The fleet action between Schley and Cervera at Santiago (*above*) resulted in one American's being killed and one wounded, while Spanish casualties were almost 500. The armistice which reached troops in the field at Puerto Rico August 13 (*below*) put an end to an almost equally bloodless campaign being waged by Major General Nelson A. Miles.

As the Closing Years of the 19th Century Approached,

SHORTLY before the armistice, Spain had asked for peace terms through the French ambassador at Washington. The United States specified three conditions: (1) that Spain give up all claim to Cuba and withdraw its forces from the island; (2) that Spain should give Puerto Rico and an island in the Ladrones, to be named later, to the United States as an indemnity; (3) that the United States should control Manila pending disposition of the Philippine Islands. The protocol of August 12 met these terms.

Peace negotiations began at Paris October 1, 1898. On December 10, the peace treaty was signed. By its chief provisions, Cuba was to be given independence and its debt assumed by Spain; Puerto Rico and Guam were ceded to the United States; the Philippine Islands were "sold" to the United States for 20 million dollars. After bitter debate, the treaty was ratified on February 6, 1899. Acquisition of the nearly one million Puerto Ricans and more than seven million Filipinos made the United States one of the imperialistic powers.

After years of endorsing self-determination for minorities, and pious support of the Monroe Doctrine, the U.S.A. suddenly appeared to be showing feet of clay. The British magazine *Punch* lost no time in preparing a barbed gibe (*opposite page*).

President McKinley wrestled long and hard with the question of the Philippines. He could have extended a protective custody over the islands, made trade agreements, and let the matter rest there. In the end, swayed by public opinion, he stated that the island group was ripe for anarchy and there was nothing left for the United States but to take over and educate, uplift, and Christianize the Filipinos.

There were sharp cries of revolt against this American descent into imperialism. In late 1898, the Anti-Imperialist League was formed in Boston. Such men as Charles Francis Adams, Carl Schurz, Grover Cleveland, William Jennings Bryan, Samuel Gompers, Andrew Carnegie, William James, and Mark Twain joined in denouncing the new American colonialism on moral, economic, and political grounds.

One immediate result of American control of the Philippines came in the form of revolt. Aguinaldo, the native leader, led his insurrectionists in proclaiming a republic in 1899. U.S. troops fought the revolutionist in a bitter guerrilla war which did not end until 1902.

In Cuba, the United States helped restore government and education, established necessary health measures, and got out, as promised. Strong political and economic ties were maintained with the island, which granted the U.S. the right to establish two naval bases on the Cuban coast.

At home, Americans took imperialism in their stride, as a right. The nation was bulging with prosperity.

Gold poured into the country from the Klondike, Alaska, and South Africa. Industry boomed, wages rose, and farm prices shot up. In 1900, McKinley rode the wave of plenty, decisively beat Bryan for the presidency, and carried in Theodore Roosevelt as Vice-President.

On December 31, 1899, the New York *World* summed up the years: "This has been a century of mechanical invention rather than of social reconstruction—a period of rapidly increasing wealth production, rather than its just distribution." America was glittering and very great. The problem of balancing material wealth with humanitarianism was one for the twentieth century.

The United States Became an Important Colonial Power

PUNCH, OR THE LONDON CHARIVARI.—August 6, 1898.

DOCTRINE AND PRACTICE.

Dame Europa (*coldly*). "TO WHOM DO I OWE THE PLEASURE OF THIS INTRUSION?"
Uncle S. "MA'AM—MY NAME IS UNCLE SAM!"
Dame Europa. "ANY RELATION OF THE LATE COLONEL MONROE?"

303

BIBLIOGRAPHY

General reference works consulted in preparing this book include the *Dictionary of American Biography, Encyclopaedia Britannica, The Encyclopedia Americana* and *The Columbia Encyclopedia*. Contemporary reports from such periodicals as *Harper's Weekly* and *The Illustrated London News* proved helpful. The bulk of the research was prepared from the books listed below.

Andrews, E. B., *History of the United States,* New York: Charles Scribner's Sons, 1916

Andrews, E. B., *The History of the Last Quarter-Century in the United States, 1870–1895,* New York: Charles Scribner's Sons, 1896

Barton, Lucy, *Historic Costume for the Stage,* Boston: Walter H. Baker Company, 1938

Beard, Mary, *A Short History of the American Labor Movement,* New York: Harcourt, Brace and Howe, 1920

Beebe, Lucius, and Charles Clegg, *The American West,* New York: E. P. Dutton and Co., Inc., 1955

Berg, Albert E., and others, *Kelly's Universal Self-Instructor,* New York: Thomas Kelly, 1891

Billington, Ray Allen, *Westward Expansion,* New York: The Macmillan Company, 1949

Butterfield, Roger, *The American Past,* New York: Simon and Schuster, 1957

Collier, John, *Indians of the Americas,* New York: New American Library, 1947

Crofutt, George A., *Crofutt's Trans-Continental Tourist's Guide,* New York: George A. Crofutt, 1873

Downey, Fairfax, *Indian-Fighting Army,* New York: Bantam Books, 1957

Freidel, Frank, *The Splendid Little War,* Boston and Toronto: Little, Brown and Company, 1958

Goodsell, Willystine, *A History of Marriage and the Family,* New York: The Macmillan Company, 1934

Hacker, Louis M., and Benjamin B. Kendrick, *The United States Since 1865,* New York: Appleton-Century-Crofts, Inc., Fourth Edition, 1949

Hicks, John D., *The American Nation,* Cambridge: Houghton Mifflin Company, Third Edition, 1955

Jensen, Oliver, *The Revolt of American Women,* New York: Harcourt, Brace and Company, 1952

Kouwenhoven, John A., *Adventures of America,* New York: Harper and Brothers, 1938

Krout, John A., *Annals of American Sport,* New Haven: Yale University Press, 1929 (The Pageant of America, Vol. 15)

Morison, Samuel Eliot, and Henry S. Commager, *The Growth of the American Republic,* New York: Oxford University Press, 1942

Mumford, Lewis, *Sticks and Stones,* New York: Dover Publications, Inc., 1955

Mumford, Lewis, *The Brown Decades,* New York: Dover Publications, Inc., 1955

Muzzey, David S., *American History,* Boston: Ginn and Company, 1917

Muzzey, David S., and John A. Krout, *American History for Colleges,* Boston: Ginn and Company, 1938

Nevins, Allan, *The Emergence of Modern America, 1865–1878,* New York: The Macmillan Company, 1927

Nevins, Allan, and Henry S. Commager, *The Pocket History of the United States,* New York: Pocket Books, Inc., 1951

Noble, Stuart G., *A History of American Education,* New York: Rinehart and Company, Inc., 1954

Robb, David M., and J. J. Garrison, *Art in the Western World,* New York: Harper and Brothers, 1935

Schlesinger, Arthur M., *The Rise of Modern America, 1865–1951,* New York: The Macmillan Company, Fourth Edition, 1951

Schlesinger, Arthur M., *The Rise of the City, 1878–1898,* New York: The Macmillan Company

Sullivan, Louis H., *The Autobiography of an Idea,* New York: Dover Publications, Inc., 1956

Tschopik, Harry, Jr., *Indians of North America,* New York: The American Museum of Natural History, 1952

Wilson, Mitchell, *American Science and Invention,* New York: Simon and Schuster, 1954

PICTURE CREDITS

Wherever possible, each individual picture credit carries the name of the artist, the source of the picture, and the date. In some cases, pictures taken from scrapbooks or files lacked this information. On the individual page, pictures are listed from left to right, top to bottom. Abbreviations used are *HW* for *Harper's Weekly*, *FLIN*, for *Frank Leslie's Illustrated Newspaper* and *ILN* for *The Illustrated London News*.

306

INDEX

309

Please remember that this is a library book,
and that it belongs only temporarily to each
person who uses it. Be considerate. Do
not write in this, or any, library book.

DATE DUE

WITHDRAWN